GOD'S WILL

for our

DAILY LIVES

The Teaching of
JESUS CHRIST

I dedicate this book to my mum.
I thank Joanne and Steph.

To contact the author, email:
witback@gmail.com

NOTE
All scripture quotes and references are from the
King James Version of the Bible, because it proves to be
the best version for consistency of wording.

Contents

WHAT THIS BOOK

IS

- Chapter one is the Christian's seven phases of spiritual development from insemination to maturity.

- Chapter two is the Christian's ongoing sacred duty, following maturity.

- Chapter three to five is the Christian's nourishment [knowledge and understanding] that is required at phase four of spiritual development, in order to progress to maturity.

- Chapter six is the Christian's supreme authority.

- Chapter seven is the Christian's defense against failing their sacred duty.

Chapter One

OUR SPIRITUAL DEVELOPMENT
Growth in God's Grace

Matthew 5:1-9.

1-2 Seeing the multitudes of people following Him, Christ went up the side of a hill, so that they all could hear Him. And when He was set, His disciples joined Him. Then He talked to the people, and taught them, saying:

Phase 1: Spiritual Insemination / Sowing

3 Blessed are the poor in spirit.

Endowed with God's favour are people who are contrite at heart, and therefore deeply and unreservedly accept Christ's gospel concerning God's eternal kingdom - that Christ died to pay the penalty for our breaking of God's law, in order to free us from the curse of God's law and make us members of His eternal kingdom. They deeply and unreservedly accept the spiritual insemination of the Truth into their heart, and consequently the responsibility of supporting and nurturing the new spiritual life that it creates within them. Ps 34:18; Isai 66:2; Matt 13:23; Rom 4:25; Gal 3:13; 1 Pet 1:23.

Christ says that the world divides into four types of people in response to His gospel: [1] the stubborn at heart, who instantly refuse it, [2] the superficial at heart, who shallowly accept it, and therefore soon abandon it, [3] the reserved at heart, who deeply yet reservedly accept it, and therefore inevitably deprive their new spiritual life of nourishment, and [4] the contrite at heart, who deeply and unreservedly accept Christ's gospel concerning God's eternal kingdom, and therefore support and nurture their new spiritual life. Lk 8:11-15.

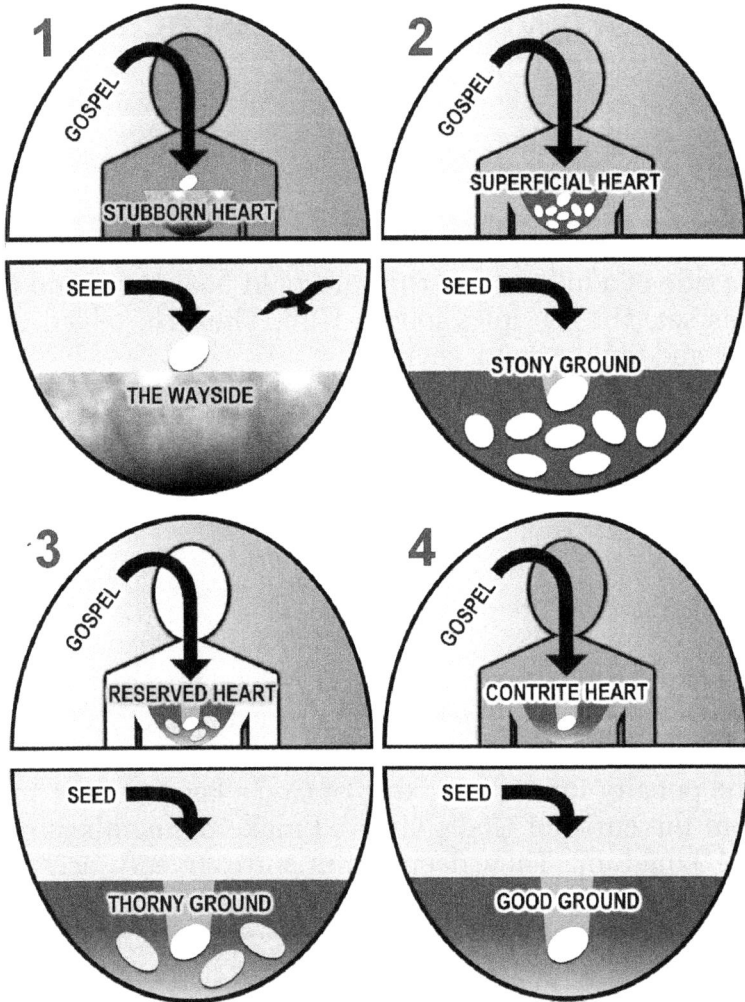

*1. Stubborn / Wayside. 2. Superficial / Stony.
3. Reserved / Thorny. 4. Contrite / Good*

Metaphorically speaking: Christ's gospel is the farmer's seed, and the world divides into four types of ground in relation to the seed: [1] the Wayside, which instantly refuses the seed, [2]

Stony Ground, which shallowly accepts the seed, and therefore soon falls away from it, [3] Thorny Ground, which deeply yet reservedly accepts the seed, and therefore inevitably deprives its plant of nourishment, and [4] Good Ground, which deeply and unreservedly accepts the seed, and therefore supports and nurtures its plant. Lk 8:5-8.

For theirs is the kingdom of heaven.

For those people who are contrite at heart [repentant], and therefore deeply and unreservedly accept [believe] Christ's gospel concerning God's eternal kingdom - that Christ died to pay the penalty for our breaking of God's law, in order to free us from the curse of God's law and make us members of His eternal kingdom - they are members of God's eternal kingdom. Mk 1:15; Jas 2:5; 2 Pet 1:11.

Metaphorically speaking: Ground that is broken at heart and deeply and unreservedly accepts the farmer's seed is Good Ground in the farmer's land.

Phase 2: Spiritual Conception / Absorption

4 Blessed are they that mourn.

Endowed with God's favour are people who, having deeply and unreservedly accepted Christ's gospel concerning God's eternal kingdom, then mourn due to Christ's gospel consuming their spiritual error. They become dispirited due to the Truth purging their heart of their previous spiritual belief. Matt 16:25; 1 Cor 5:7; Heb 9:14.

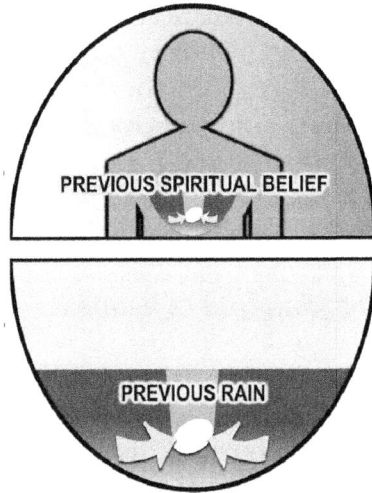

Contrite at Heart / Good Ground

Metaphorically speaking: Good Ground grieves due to the farmer's seed within it consuming its previous rain, whereas Stony Ground and Thorny Ground do not.

For they shall be comforted.

For those people who mourn due to Christ's gospel - the Truth - consuming their previous spiritual belief, they will be comforted by the Spirit of Truth when they are filled with knowledge and understanding specifically from Christ's teaching. Jn 15:26.

Phase 3: Spiritual Implantation / Germination

5 Blessed are the meek.

Endowed with God's favour are people who, having mourned due to Christ's gospel consuming their previous spiritual belief, then become fully and exclusively submissive at heart to the fundamental truth of Christ's gospel - that all people must now be reconciled to God by faith in Christ as the sacrificial Lamb, <u>and</u> regarded as right in God's sight by faithfulness to Christ as the resurrected Lord. They become fully and exclusively submissive at heart to the Truth, Christ, God's Word incarnate - the New Testament to God's will. Rom 4:25; 5:10; 6:4; 7:4; Heb 5:9; Jas 1:21.

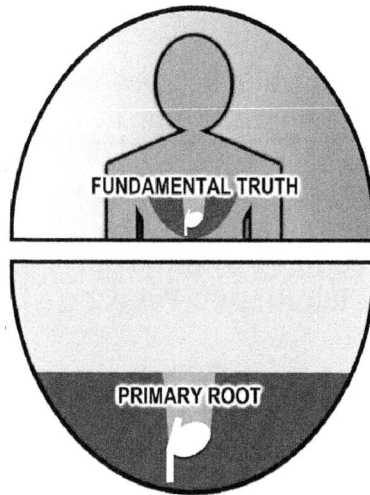

Contrite at Heart / Good Ground

Metaphorically speaking: Good Ground fully and exclusively submits to the primary root of the farmer's seed, whereas Stony Ground and Thorny Ground do not.

For they shall inherit the earth.

For those people who are fully and exclusively submissive at heart to the fundamental truth of Christ's gospel - that all people must now be reconciled to God by faith in Christ as the sacrificial Lamb, <u>and</u> regarded as right in God's sight by faithfulness to Christ as the resurrected Lord - they will reign with Christ during His future millennial reign on this temporary earth and subsequent eternal reign on the earth to come. Rev 20:6; 21:1.

Phase 4: Spiritual Gestation / Nourishment

6 Blessed are they, which do hunger, and thirst after righteousness.

Endowed with God's favour are people who, having become fully and exclusively submissive at heart to the fundamental truth of Christ's gospel, then desire knowledge and understanding - spiritual food and water - concerning God's will, which is required to support and nurture a new spiritual life. They desire to be filled with the Spirit of graciousness and truth. Jn 1:14 & 17; Heb 10:29; 1 Pet 2:2-3.

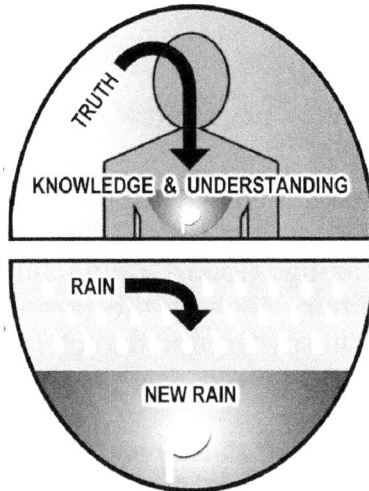

Contrite at Heart / Good Ground

Metaphorically speaking: Good Ground needs to be filled with new rain, which is required to support and nurture a plant, whereas Stony Ground and Thorny Ground do not.

For they shall be filled.

For those people who genuinely desire knowledge and understanding concerning God's will, they will be satisfied with the knowledge and understanding specifically from Christ's teaching - first with the knowledge, and then with the understanding contained within that knowledge. Jn 14:17; 17:17.

Phase 5: Spiritual Talking / Leaf Bearing

7 Blessed are the merciful.

Endowed with God's favour are people who, having been satisfied with the knowledge concerning God's will specifically from Christ's teaching, then support and nurture their new spiritual life's potential to consistently bear forgiveness and compassion - mercy - towards all people irrespective of persons. They consistently produce a sound testimony to God's will.

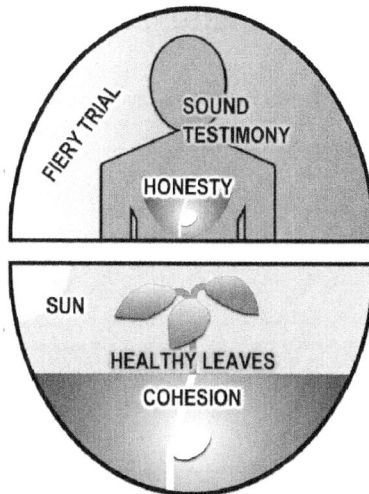

Contrite at Heart / Good Ground

Metaphorically speaking: Good Ground supports and nurtures its plant's potential to consistently bear healthy leaves, whereas Stony Ground and Thorny Ground do not.

For they shall obtain mercy.

For those people who support and nurture their new spiritual life's potential to consistently bear forgiveness and compassion towards all people irrespective of persons, they will obtain forgiveness and compassion from God.

People who fail to support and nurture their new spiritual life's potential to consistently bear forgiveness and compassion towards all people irrespective of persons, do so because they are full of opinions concerning God's will. Therefore, they have not become fully submissive at heart to the fundamental truth of Christ's gospel. Nor have they actually been satisfied with the knowledge concerning God's will specifically from Christ's teaching. Hence, they are immediately offended when the fiery trial from God comes upon them for the sake of their initial testimony. They soon thereafter abandon Christ's gospel concerning God's eternal kingdom. And the gospel then disintegrates within them. Matt 13:20-21; Mk 4:16-17; Lk 8:13; Heb 12:7.

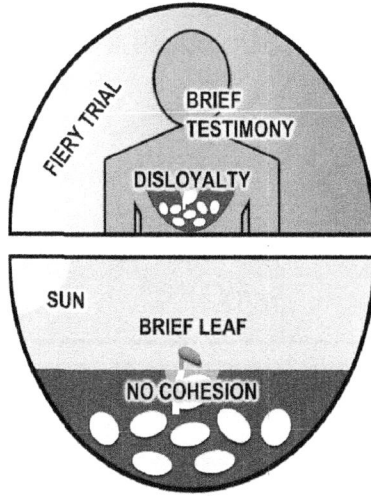

Superficial at Heart / Stony Ground

Metaphorically speaking: Stony Ground fails to support and nurture its plant's potential to consistently bear leaves, because it is full of stones. Therefore, it has not fully submitted to the primary root of the farmer's seed. Nor has it actually been filled with new rain. Hence it is immediately scorched when the heat from the sun comes upon it for the sake of its initial leaf. It soon thereafter falls away from the farmer's seed. And the seed then decomposes within it. Matt 13:5-6; Mk 4:5-6; Lk 8:6.

Phase 6: Spiritual Living / Fruit Bearing

8 Blessed are the pure at heart.

Endowed with God's favour are people who, having been satisfied with the understanding concerning God's will specifically from Christ's teaching, then go on in time to nurture their new spiritual life's potential to actually bear kindness and consideration - love - towards all people irrespective of persons. They actually produce a good example of God's will. Matt 13:23; Mk 4:20; Lk 8:15.

Contrite at Heart / Good Ground

Metaphorically speaking: Good Ground nurtures its plant's potential to actually bear good fruit, whereas Stony Ground and Thorny Ground do not. Matt 13:8; Mk 4:8; Lk 8:8.

For they shall see God.

For those people who nurture their new spiritual life's potential to actually bear kindness and consideration towards all people irrespective of persons, they will see Christ: God incarnate. Jn 1:1 & 14; 1 Jn 3:2-3.

People who fail to nurture their new spiritual life's potential to actually bear kindness and consideration towards all people irrespective of persons, do so because they also nurture feelings that are contrary to God's will. They have not become exclusively submissive at heart to the fundamental truth of Christ's gospel. Nor have they actually been satisfied with the understanding concerning God's will specifically from Christ's teaching. Hence, the growth of their new spiritual life is gradually retarded by the cares of the world, the deceitfulness of riches, and the lust for pleasures of temporal life. They deprive their new spiritual life of nourishment. And they inevitably produce a bad example of God's will. Matt 13:22; Mk 4:18-19; Lk 8:14.

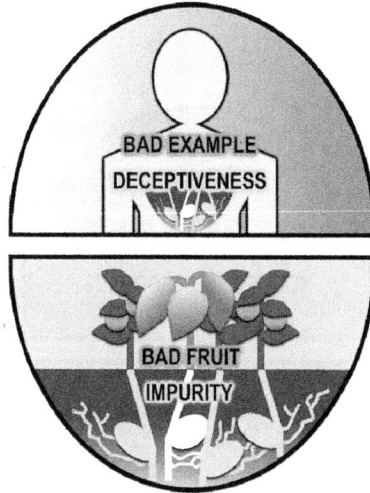

Reserved at Heart / Thorny Ground

Metaphorically speaking: Thorny Ground fails to nurture its plant's potential to actually bear good fruit, because it also nurtures thorn seeds. It has not exclusively submitted to the primary root of the farmer's seed. Nor has it actually been filled with new rain. Hence the growth of its plant is gradually choked by thorns. It deprives its plant of nourishment. And it inevitably bears bad fruit. Matt 13:7; Mk 4:7; Lk 8:7.

Phase 7: Spiritual Teaching / Seed Bearing

9 Blessed are the peacemakers.

Endowed with God's favour are people who, having been

satisfied with both the knowledge and understanding concerning God's will specifically from Christ's teaching, then go on to nurture their new spiritual life to maturity - completeness / perfection - capable of teaching the Truth to others. They produce sound teaching concerning God's will - that God's subjects <u>must</u> bear kindness and consideration towards all people irrespective of persons, as per Christ's teaching. Jn 15:17; 2 Tim 3:17; Heb 13:21; Jas 1:4; 2 Jn 1:9.

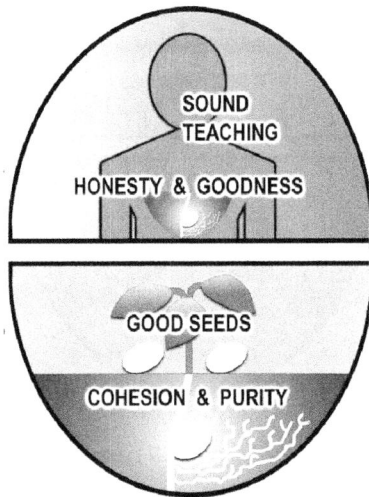

Contrite at Heart / Good Ground

Metaphorically speaking: Good Ground goes on to nurture its plant to maturity, capable of bearing good seed, whereas Stony Ground and Thorny Ground do not.

For they shall be called the children of God.

For those people who nurture their new spiritual life to maturity and are capable of teaching others the Truth - that God's subjects <u>must</u> bear kindness and consideration towards all people irrespective of persons - they are thoroughly conformed to God's Image, His Son [the Seed].

For Christ is the Word of God made flesh, the Truth from God. Jn 1:1 & 14; 14:6; Rom 8:29.

Summary

We must deeply and unreservedly accept Christ's gospel concerning God's eternal kingdom, in order for our new spiritual life to grow in God's graciousness - develop spiritually. Ps 34:18; Rom 10:10; Prov 3:5; Jas 4:8; 2 Pet 3:18.

Chapter Two

OUR SACRED DUTY

Service to God

Matthew 5:10-16.

Having just outlined the seven phases of spiritual development, Christ then proceeded to define our sacred duty on this temporary earth, saying:

Our Duty to Endure Accusation Due to God's Will

> *10 Blessed are they, which are persecuted for righteousness' sake.*

Endowed with God's favour are people who endure false accusations fired at them by the devil because of their testament to God's will. Eph 6:16.

Metaphorically speaking: Good Ground endures fiery darts fired at it by the farmer's enemy because of its plant.

> *For theirs is the kingdom of heaven.*

For those people who endure false accusations fired at them because of their testament to God's will, they are members of God's eternal kingdom. 2 Pet 1:11.

Our Duty to Endure Persecution Due to God's Will

11 Blessed are you when men shall revile you, and persecute you, and shall say all manner of evil against you falsely, for My sake.

Endowed with God's favour are you, when you endure unjustifiable criticism, victimization and slander, inflicted upon you by worldly hearted people because of your new spiritual life, that is, because of Christ, God's Word incarnate - the New Testament to God's will - growing within you spiritually. Gal 2:20.

Metaphorically speaking: Good Ground endures the rain, floods, and winds, inflicted upon it by the world for the sake of its plant. Matt 7:25.

For you who endure unjustifiable criticism, victimization, and slander, inflicted upon you because of your new spiritual life, you will be greatly rewarded when Christ returns. Matt 16:27; Lk 9:26; 1 Pet 4:14.

Our Duty to Accept Suffering Due to God's Will

12 Rejoice and be exceedingly glad. For great is your reward in heaven. For so persecuted they the prophets which were before you.

Be joyous and extremely grateful for whatever suffering you may experience because of God's will. Don't be discouraged. For all the prophets before you were persecuted in exactly the same way. By accepting suffering due to God's will, you partake in Christ's sufferings, bearing the consequence of your compliance with God's will [your cross], as Christ bore the consequence of His compliance with God's will [His cross].

Hence you will also partake in the glory to come. Lk 9:23-26; Rom 8:17; 1 Pet 4:13.

Our Duty to Produce a Testimony to God's Will

13 You are the salt of the earth: but if the salt have lost his savour, wherewith shall it be salted? It is thenceforth good for nothing, but to be cast out, and to be trodden under foot of men.

You are the salt of the earth as long as you bear a savour of knowledge concerning God's will. To those who are saved, you should consistently bear a savour of knowledge concerning reconciliation to God, which affirms their reconciliation to God. To those who perish, you should consistently bear a savour of knowledge concerning separation from God, which affirms their separation from God. 2 Cor 2:14-17.

But if you do not consistently bear a savour of knowledge [salt] concerning God's will, then you are good for nothing other than to be used as intellectual underpinning by opinionated people.

Metaphorically speaking: Ground that does not consistently bear leaves from the farmer's seed is good for nothing other than to be trodden under foot by worldly minded people.

Therefore set apart in your mind as complete the Lord Jesus Christ, God's Word incarnate - the New Testament to God's will - so as to ensure that you consistently produce a sound testimony to God's will, and thereby ensure that you remain a profitable servant of God, destined to inherit salvation from the lake of fire. Matt 25:30; 1 Pet 3:15.

Our Duty to Produce an Example of God's Will

14-16 You are the light of the world. A city that is set on a hill cannot be hid. Neither do men light a candle, and put it under a bushel, but on a candlestick; and it giveth light unto all that are in the house. Let your light so shine before men, that they may see your good works, and glorify your Father which is in heaven at Christ's return.

You are the light of the world as long as you bear understanding concerning God's will. To all those around you at any given time, you should bear understanding concerning rightness in God's sight - that God's subjects <u>must</u> bear kindness and consideration [love] towards all people irrespective of persons, as per Christ's teaching. Philip 2:15.

But if you do not actually bear understanding [light] concerning God's will, then you are good for nothing other than to have your life used for emotional warmth by sentimental people. Jn 15:6.

Metaphorically speaking: Ground that does not actually bear fruit from the farmer's seed is good for nothing other than to have its plant burned by worldly hearted people.

Therefore set apart in your heart as complete the Lord Jesus Christ, God's Word incarnate - the New Testament to God's will - so as to ensure that you actually produce a good example of God's will, and thereby ensure that you are a profitable servant of God, destined to see the Saviour. Matt 5:8; 1 Pet 3:15.

Summary

We must consistently produce a testament to God's will, in order to fulfil our service to God - our sacred duty. Philip 2:15; 1 Pet 2:16; 4:13; Rom 12:1; Lk 17:10.

Chapter Three

OUR RIGHTNESS IN LIFE

Righteousness

Matthew 5:17-48.

Pre-empting our misunderstanding of the Law, following His teaching concerning who is endowed with God's favour [blessed], Christ proceeded to explain our daily righteousness, saying:

Rightness Concerning the Mosaic Law

> *17-18 Think not that I am come to destroy the law, or the prophets: I am not come to destroy, but to fulfil. For verily I say unto you, Till heaven and earth pass, one jot or one tittle shall in no wise pass from the law, till all be fulfilled.*

Don't think that Christ came to destroy the Law of Moses. For the purpose of the Mosaic Law - primarily the Ten Commandments - is to convince people of their unrighteousness, their sin, in order to humble them so that they may deeply and unreservedly accept into their heart, Christ's gospel concerning God's eternal kingdom. Therefore not even the smallest part of the Mosaic Law will be done away with until all the preaching of Christ's gospel is completed.

However, the Mosaic Law itself cannot enable people to bear fruit unto God. Christ's gospel concerning God's eternal kingdom, which contains God's Spirit of grace, is required to change a person's inherently self-centered nature so that they can bear the fruit of God's Spirit, to God's glory.

Hence Christ came to fulfil the righteousness of the Mosaic Law, in that He came to complete its righteous work in people. By condemning unrighteousness to death within His physical body, by the presence of God's Spirit within His spiritual core during His death and resurrection to life, Christ has made it possible for unrighteousness to be condemned to death within our physical bodies, by the presence of God's Spirit within our spiritual cores. Matt 24:14; Rom 3:19-21; 7:4-6; 8:3-5 & 9-11; Gal 2:16; 3:24; 2 Pet 1:4.

Metaphorically speaking: The sower did not come to destroy the plough. For the purpose of the plough is to cut furrows in the ground in order to break it, so that it may deeply and unreservedly accept the farmer's seed into its heart. Therefore the plough will not be done away with until all the sowing of the seed is completed. However, the plough itself cannot enable the ground to bear fruit unto the farmer. The farmer's seed, which contains the essence of life, is required to change the ground's inherently lifeless nature so that it can bear fruit to the farmer's glory. Hence the sower came to complete the righteous work of the plough, in that he came to sow the seed deep into the ground broken by the plough.

The righteous work of the Mosaic Law is completed by Christ in people who deeply and unreservedly accept His gospel concerning God's eternal kingdom, in that Christ, God's Word incarnate - the New Testament to God's will - grows within those people and bears love towards all people irrespective of persons, to God's glory. Hence Christ is the end of the Mosaic Law concerning God's will, for people who deeply and unreservedly accept His gospel concerning God's eternal kingdom. Rom 8:1-4; 10:4; Heb 1:1-2; 2:1-3; 9:15.

Metaphorically speaking: The righteous work of the plough is ultimately completed by the farmer's seed in ground that deeply and unreservedly accepts it, in that it grows within that ground and bears good fruit to the farmer's glory. Hence the farmer's seed is the end of the plough concerning the farmer's will, for ground that deeply and unreservedly accepts the farmer's seed.

The Mosaic Law was our teacher. It was the schoolmaster to bring us to Christ, so that we might be regarded as right, justified in God's sight, through living in accordance with faith in Christ. But after that faith has come, we are no longer under a schoolmaster: the Mosaic Law. For we are all the children of God through living in accordance with our faith in Christ, apart from the Mosaic Law. Indeed, Christ, God's Word incarnate - the New Testament to God's will - does not take root in whoever continues under the authority of the Mosaic Law after accepting Christ's gospel. For continued subjection to the forcefulness of the Mosaic Law, prevents people from adhering to Christ's gospel of the kingdom. Rom 3:28; 7:4-7; Gal 3:24-26; 5:4.

Metaphorically speaking: The plough cuts furrows in the ground, so that the ground might be justified by its depth of earth for the farmer's seed. But after the seed has been accepted deep into its heart, the ground is no longer subject to the plough. For then the ground's relationship to the farmer is by its depth of earth for the farmer's seed, irrespective of the plough. Indeed, the farmer's seed does not take root in ground that continues under the force of the plough after accepting the seed. For continued subjection to the force of the plough, prevents the ground from adhering to the farmer's seed.

The just shall live by faith, that is, they shall have spiritual life in accordance with their depth and unreservedness of conviction for God's Word, apart from the Mosaic Law. But if anyone draws back from God's Word, back to the Mosaic Law or whatever, God's soul shall have no pleasure in that person. They draw back to spiritual death and ultimately eternal punishment in the lake of fire. They do not believe to the saving of their soul. They fall from grace, from the Spirit of God's graciousness contained within Christ's gospel of the kingdom. Jn 1:14-17; Rom 1:16-17; Gal 5:4; Heb 10:29 & 38-39; Lk 16:16.

Metaphorically speaking: Good Ground has life in accordance with its depth of earth for the farmer's seed within it, apart from the plough. But if any ground falls away from the seed, due to the plough or whatever, the essence of life contained within the seed shall have no pleasure in that ground. That ground falls away to unfruitfulness and ultimately devastation by fire. It falls from the essence of life contained within the farmer's seed. Heb 12:15a.

The letter of the Mosaic Law kills, but the Spirit of graciousness gives life. Now the Lord Jesus Christ is that Spirit, and where the Spirit of the Lord is, there is liberty from the authority of the Mosaic Law. Jn 1:14-17; 2 Cor 3:6 & 17; Philip 1:19; Lk 16:16.

For by grace - the Spirit of graciousness dwelling in your heart, condemning your unrighteousness to death in your flesh, and working to do righteousness - are you saved through faith in Christ. And it is not of yourselves. It - the Spirit of graciousness - is the gift of God. It is not of works pertaining to the flesh, lest any man should boast. For we are God's workmanship, created in Christ Jesus to do good works pertaining to God's Spirit of grace, which God has before ordained that we should walk in. Rom 5:15; 8:9-14; 1 Cor 1:4; Eph 2:8-10; 3:7-8; 4:7; Philip 2:13; Heb 10:29.

There is therefore now no condemnation to them that are in Christ Jesus, who walk not after the flesh, but after the Spirit of graciousness. For the law of the Spirit of life in Christ Jesus - i.e. the command to love one another out of God's Spirit of graciousness - makes us free from the law of sin and death, the Mosaic Law, which convicts of sin and therefore condemns to spiritual death. Rom 8:1-2; Gal 5:18; Jn 8:31-32.

After John the Baptist was put in prison, Jesus came into Galilee, preaching the gospel of the kingdom of God. For the Mosaic Law and the prophets were until John the Baptist. But since that time - since the end of John's ministry - the kingdom of God is preached, and everyone presses into it. And it is easier for heaven and earth to pass, than for the tiniest part of the Mosaic Law to fail. For the Law is perfect, converting the soul, making wise the simple, with the intent of leading people to Christ and the kingdom of God. Matt 11:12-13; Mk 1:14; Lk 16:16-17; Ps 19:7; Gal 3:24.

Rightness Concerning Works of Faith

19 Whosoever therefore shall break one of these least commandments, and shall teach men so, he shall be called the least in the kingdom of heaven; but whosoever shall do and teach them, the same shall be called great in the kingdom of heaven.

Since the righteous work of the Mosaic Law is completed by Christ in people who deeply and unreservedly accept His gospel - in that Christ, God's Word incarnate, grows within those people and bears love towards all people irrespective of persons to God's glory - whoever deeply and unreservedly accepts Christ's gospel and yet consistently breaks the least of His following commands, and teaches others to do likewise, they will be deemed the least profitable servants in God's eternal kingdom. But whoever deeply and unreservedly accepts Christ's gospel and consistently does all of His following commands, and teaches others to do likewise, they will be deemed the most profitable servants in God's eternal kingdom. For those who consistently break the least of Christ's following commands, and teach others to do likewise, they fail to nurture their new spiritual life to its full potential, whereas those who consistently do all of Christ's following commands, and teach others to do likewise, they succeed in nurturing their new spiritual life to its full potential. Nonetheless, all who deeply and unreservedly accept Christ's gospel concerning God's eternal kingdom are profitable to God, bearing love towards all people irrespective of persons, some a hundred-fold, some sixty-fold, some thirty-fold. Matt 13:23.

Metaphorically speaking: Ground that deeply and unreservedly accepts the farmer's seed and yet fails to nurture its plant to its full potential, that ground will be deemed the least profitable Good Ground in the farmer's land. But ground that deeply and unreservedly accepts the farmer's seed and succeeds in nurturing its plant to its full potential, that ground will be deemed the most profitable Good Ground in the farmer's land. Nonetheless, all ground that deeply and unreservedly accepts the farmer's seed is Good Ground, in that it is profitable to the farmer, bearing good fruit, some a hundred-fold, some sixty-fold, some thirty-fold. Matt 13:8.

Christ has redeemed you from the curse of the Mosaic Law for the purpose of consistently producing a testament on earth to God's will, to His glory. Christ bought you with His blood in order to free you from slavery to human will, from slavery to unrighteousness [sin], and to make you a servant of God's will, a servant of righteousness. You are now God's servant, and your sacred duty on this temporary earth is to consistently produce a spiritual life that is a testament to God's will, to His glory. Gal 3:13; Rom 7:4-6; Eph 2:10; 1 Cor 6:20; Titus 2:14.

Metaphorically speaking: You are now the farmer's ground, and your purpose is to consistently produce a plant that is a testament to the soundness of the farmer's seed, to the farmer's glory. You are God's builder, and your work is to consistently produce a house that is a testament to the soundness of God's foundation, to God's glory. 1 Cor 3:9.

According to the graciousness of God which was given to him as a wise master builder, the apostle Paul laid the foundation upon which all Christians must build their testament to God's will, to His glory. Paul warns all to mind how they build upon the foundation he laid. For no other foundation can be laid on top of it. Every Christian must build a testament to God's will directly upon the foundation that Paul laid, the fundamental truth of Christ's gospel - that all people must now be reconciled to God by faith in Christ as the sacrificial Lamb, and regarded as right in God's sight by faithfulness to Christ as the resurrected Lord. This fundamental truth was first spoken by Christ in person, and confirmed to us by those who heard Him, namely, the writers of the New Testament. 1 Cor 3:10-11; Heb 1:1-2; 2:1-3; 9:15; 2 Cor 3:6.

Furthermore, every Christian's testament must suffer false accusations [fiery darts] which God allows the devil to fire at them in order to reveal the value of their testament, whether it is honourable or dishonourable to God. Then all will later be rewarded accordingly at the judgment seat of Christ. Eph 6:16; 2 Cor 5:9-10; Rev 12:10-11.

People who consistently comply with all of Christ's following commands, and teach others to do likewise, they consistently do honourable work. They produce a valuable testament to God's will. They consistently produce a testimony, example, and teaching, worth gold, silver, and precious stones, respectively. Such work will endure the accusations from the devil, and will thereby be revealed as honourable to God. Those who produce such valuable testament are presently deemed the most profitable servants in God's eternal kingdom, and they will later be greatly rewarded at the judgment seat of Christ. Moreover, as profitable servants of God, they will be saved from the lake of fire. 1 Cor 3:12-14.

Conversely, people who consistently break the least of Christ's following commands, and teach others to do likewise, even if they consistently do all of the rest of them, and teach others to do likewise, they consistently do dishonourable work. They produce a poor testament to God's will. They consistently produce a testimony, example, and teaching, worth wood, hay, and stubble, respectively. Such work will not endure the accusations from the devil, and will thereby be revealed as dishonourable to God. Those who produce such poor testament are presently deemed the least profitable servants in God's eternal kingdom, and they will later suffer loss at the judgment seat of Christ. In spite of this, they are still profitable servants of God, and as such they will still be saved from the lake of fire, albeit through continual suffering due to accusations from the devil [fiery darts]. For even though they produce a poor testament to God's will, they keep on producing it, despite it being repeatedly burned up by fiery trial. So they still consistently produce a testament to God's will, to His glory. 1 Cor 3:15; Jn 15:2; 2 Tim 2:20-21.

Metaphorically speaking: Ground deemed the least profitable Good Ground in the farmer's land is still Good Ground. For even though it produces a poor plant, it keeps on producing it, despite it being repeatedly burned up by the farmer's enemy. So it still consistently produces a plant that serves as a testament to the soundness of the farmer's seed, to his glory.

> *20 For I say unto you, That except your righteousness shall exceed the righteousness of the scribes and Pharisees you shall in no case enter the kingdom of heaven.*

For although no person is redeemed from the curse of the Mosaic Law by righteous works such as silver or gold, but solely by the precious blood of Christ, under no circumstance will anyone actually inherit God's eternal kingdom unless they consistently produce a testament to God's will which exceeds that of the scribes and Pharisees. For Christ redeems people from the curse of the Mosaic Law for the very purpose of them consistently producing a testament to God's will, His righteousness. The Pharisees however unwittingly worked at producing a testament to their own righteousness in keeping the Law. Also, by keeping the unproductive works of the Mosaic Law, and teaching others to do likewise, they failed to submit themselves to God's will apart from the Mosaic Law i.e. Christ, God's Word incarnate - the New Testament to God's will. Thus they failed to fulfil the righteousness of the Mosaic Law. For Christ is the end of the Mosaic Law concerning righteousness. Christ commands that we bear kindness and consideration [love] towards all people irrespective of persons, as He did. Love works no harm to his neighbour. Therefore, love is the fulfilling of the Mosaic Law. 1 Pet 1:18-19; Rom 9:31

-32; 10:1-4; Gal 3:11; Philip 3:9; Jn 15:12; Rom 7:4, 13:10.

Rightness Concerning Christ's Law

> *21 Ye have heard that it was said of them of old time, Thou shalt not kill; and whoever shall kill shall be in danger of the judgment.*
> *22 But I [Christ] say unto you, That whosoever is angry with his brother without a cause shall be in danger of the judgment: and whosoever shall say to his brother, Raca, shall be in danger of the council: but whosoever shall say, Thou fool, shall be in danger of hell-fire.*

The scribes and Pharisees taught that in Old Testament times God spoke to the forefathers by the Mosaic Law and the prophets, saying that no person is to kill another person, and that whoever does so will themselves be in danger of being put to physical death. They were right to teach this, for indeed God did say it! But the Pharisees mistakenly believed that God was merely declaring the act of killing to be unrighteous, when in fact God's intention was that by this commandment people would learn that they are inherently self-righteous at heart.

God added the Mosaic Law to the Old Testament in order to convince people of their unrighteousness, of their sin, with the intent of humbling them so that they may deeply and unreservedly accept Christ's gospel concerning His eternal kingdom. Heb 1:1; Exod 20:13; Num 35:30; Gal 3:19 & 24-25; 1 Tim 1:8.

But to you who have already accepted His gospel, Christ - the mediator of the New Testament to God's will - says that if you are angry with a fellow human being without a justifiable cause, you will be in danger of spiritual death on this temporary earth. If you call a fellow human being worthless, you will be in danger of being convinced by the Mosaic Law as a sinner. And if you call a fellow human being a fool, you will be in danger of spiritual death in the lake of fire. Gal 3:24-25; Heb 1:1-2; 2:1-3; 9:15; 10:28-29; Jas 2:9; Matt 25:30; Rev 20:14.

For whoever is angry with a fellow human being without a justifiable reason, gratifies the unrighteous lust of their flesh: self-indulgence. Whoever calls a fellow human being worthless, gratifies the unrighteous lust of their eyes: covetousness. And whoever calls a fellow human being a fool, gratifies their unrighteous pride of life: self-importance. All of which is unrighteous affection for the world: worldliness. And worldliness is enmity to God. 1 Jn 2:16; Jas 4:4.

> *23-26 Therefore if you bring your gift to the altar, and there remember that your brother has ought against you, leave there your gift before the altar, and go your way: first be reconciled to your brother, and then come and offer your gift. Agree with your adversary quickly, while you are in the way with him; lest at any time the adversary deliver you to the judge, and the judge deliver you to the officer, and you be cast into prison. Verily I say unto you, You will by no means come out thence, till you have paid the uttermost farthing.*

Therefore, if while offering praise in prayer you remember that a fellow human being has any justifiable complaint against you, then leave off from offering God praise until you are first reconciled with that person: your adversary. For God does not heed those who have partiality in their heart. He only looks to those who are contrite at heart, and who tremble at His Word. Heb 13:15; Ps 66:18; Isia 66:2; 1 Pet 3:12; 1 Jn 3:22-23.

Be reconciled - make peace - with anyone who has a justifiable complaint against you as soon as possible, preferably while you are still together, in case the devil [the adversary] delivers you to Christ [the judge] before you have another opportunity to be reconciled, and then Christ in turn delivers you to His representative angel [the officer], and he, the angel of the Lord, then places you into the devil's custody. For assuredly you will by no means come out of the devil's custody until you have paid the price - atoned in full - according to your unjustness. Eph 4:26-27; 1 Pet 5:8; 1 Cor 5:5; 11:32.

> *27 Ye have heard that it was said by them of old time, Thou shalt not commit adultery:*
> *28 But I say unto you, That whosoever looketh on a woman to lust after her hath committed adultery with her already in his heart.*

The scribes and Pharisees taught that in Old Testament times God spoke to our forefathers by the Mosaic Law and the prophets, saying that no person is to commit adultery. They were right to teach this, for indeed God did say it! But the Pharisees mistakenly believed that God was merely declaring the act of adultery to be unrighteous, when in fact God's intention was that by this commandment people would learn that they are inherently unremorseful at heart.

God added the Mosaic Law to the Old Testament in order to convince people of their unrighteousness, with the intent of humbling them so that they may deeply and unreservedly accept Christ's gospel concerning His eternal kingdom. Exod 20:14; Gal 3:19 & 24-25.

But to you who have already accepted His gospel, Christ - the mediator of the New Testament to God's will - says that if you look at a woman lustfully, that is, with the desire to physically have her for your own selfish gratification, you have committed spiritual adultery with her already in your heart.

For whoever lusts after a woman, loves the things of the world [the flesh] more than the things of God [the Spirit], and thereby commits spiritual adultery against God. Gal 3:24-25;

Heb 9:15; Jas 4:4.

> *29-30 And if thy right eye offend thee, pluck it out, and cast it from thee: for it is profitable for thee that one of thy members should perish, and not that thy whole body should be cast into hell. And if thy right hand offend thee, cut it off, and cast it from thee: for it is profitable for thee that one of thy members should perish, and not that thy whole body should be cast into hell.*

Therefore ruthlessly remove from your life whatever causes you to gratify the lust of your flesh which is self-indulgence, the lust of your eyes which is covetousness, or your pride of life which is self-importance, and thereby causes you to commit spiritual adultery against God. For it is better to sacrifice the things of the flesh, which are temporary, than to lose your very soul, which is eternal. 1 Jn 2:16; Prov 6:32; Mk 8:36; Lk 9:25; 1 Cor 9:27; Matt 25:30.

> *31 It hath been said, Whosoever shall put away his wife, let him give her a writing of divorcement:*
> *32 But I say unto you, That whosoever shall put away his wife, saving for the cause of fornication, causeth her to commit adultery: and whosoever shall marry her that is divorced committeth adultery.*

The scribes and Pharisees taught that Moses said that whoever divorces his wife must give her a writing of divorcement stating a justifiable reason. They were right to teach this, for indeed Moses did say it! But the Pharisees mistakenly believed that God was merely declaring divorce without a justifiable reason to be unrighteous, when in fact God's intention was that by this saying people would learn that they are inherently defiant at heart.

God added the Mosaic Law to the Old Testament in order to convince people of their unrighteousness, with the intent of humbling them so that they may deeply and unreservedly accept Christ's gospel concerning His eternal kingdom. Deut 24:1; Gal 3:19 & 24-25.

But to you who have already accepted His gospel, Christ - the mediator of the New Testament to God's will - says that if you divorce your wife without a justifiable reason, and then sexually join i.e. marry, with another person, you thereby break your former physical joining, your former marriage, that God has ordained. Likewise, if a woman divorces her husband without a justifiable reason, and then sexually joins with another person, she breaks her former marriage that God has ordained. Moreover, whoever sexually joins with a divorced person partakes in the breaking of their former marriage that God has ordained. Gal 3:24-25; Heb 9:15; Matt 19:4-9; Mk 10:11-12; 1 Cor 7:10-11.

For whoever breaks or partakes in the breaking of a physical joining, a marriage, ordained by God, opposes God's will in favour of their own, whether it be a person who divorces their spouse without a justifiable reason, or one who marries a divorced person.

The only justifiable reason for divorce is sexual unfaithfulness. For a spouse who has been sexually unfaithful has already sexually joined with another person, and thereby already broken the marriage that God had ordained. Matt 5:32.

However, in the case of a physical joining that God has not ordained, the unequal marriage of a true Christian - who lives in accordance with Christ's teaching - with a non-Christian, if the non-Christian is happy to dwell with the true Christian in the marriage, then the Christian should remain married to them. But if the non-Christian departs from the physical joining, then the Christian is free to divorce and physically join - marry - with another true Christian. 1 Cor 7:12-15; 2 Cor 6:14.

33 Again, ye have heard that it hath been said by them of old time, Thou shalt not forswear thyself, but shalt perform unto the Lord thine oaths:

34-37 But I say unto you, Swear not at all; neither by heaven; for it is God's throne: Nor by the earth; for it is his footstool: neither by Jerusalem; for it is the city of the great King. Neither shalt thou swear by thy head, because thou canst not make one hair white or black. But let your communication be, Yea, yea; Nay, nay: for whatsoever is more than these cometh of evil.

Again, the scribes and Pharisees taught that in Old Testament times God said to our forefathers that no person is to commit perjury. Again, they were right to teach this, for indeed God did say it! But again, the Pharisees mistakenly believed that God was merely declaring perjury to be unrighteous, when in fact God's intention was that by this commandment people would learn that they are inherently deceitful at heart.

God added the Mosaic Law to the Old Testament in order to convince people of their unrighteousness, with the intent of humbling them so that they may deeply and unreservedly accept Christ's gospel concerning His eternal kingdom. Num 30:1-2; Gal 3:19 & 24-25.

But to you who have already accepted His gospel, Christ - the mediator of the New Testament to God's will - says that you are not to swear at all, not even by your own head. You are merely to say, Yes or No, and mean it. For since God owns everything, and you are powerless to make even one hair on your head actually turn white or black, anything more than Yes or No is a lie that arises out of self-centeredness, which is evil. Heb 9:15.

38 Ye have heard that it hath been said, An eye for an eye, and a tooth for a tooth:

39-42 But I say unto you, That ye resist not evil:

but whosoever shall smite thee on thy right cheek, turn to him the other also. And if any man will sue thee at the law, and take away thy coat, let him have thy cloak also. And whosoever shall compel thee to go a mile, go with him twain. Give to him that asketh thee, and from him that would borrow of thee turn not thou away.

The scribes and Pharisees taught that God said to retaliate when wronged. Again, they were right to teach this, for indeed God did say it! But again, the Pharisees mistakenly believed that God was merely declaring retaliation to be righteous, when in fact God's intention was that by this commandment people would learn that they are inherently vengeful at heart.

God added the Mosaic Law to the Old Testament in order to convince people of their unrighteousness, with the intent of humbling them so that they may deeply and unreservedly accept Christ's gospel concerning His eternal kingdom. Lev 24:19-20; Gal 3:19 & 24-25.

But to you who have already accepted His gospel, Christ - the mediator of the New Testament to God's will - says that you are not to retaliate when wronged. Instead, you are to overcome self-centeredness [evil] with graciousness [good]. For it is God's will that His children are always innocent of wrongdoing and inoffensive towards all people irrespective of persons, so as to be seen by comparison to reprove the condemnatory words and harmful deeds of the unrighteous. Whoever opposes another person for their own benefit opposes God's will in favour of their own. Gal 3:24-25; Heb 9:15; Rom 12:21; Philip 2:15.

43 Ye have heard that it hath been said, Thou shalt love thy neighbour, and hate thine enemy.
44-45 But I say unto you, Love your enemies, bless them that curse you, do good to them that hate you, and pray for them which despitefully use you, and

persecute you; That ye may be the children of your Father which is in heaven: for he maketh his sun to rise on the evil and on the good, and sendeth rain on the just and on the unjust.

The scribes and Pharisees taught that God said to love your friends and hate your enemies. They sincerely thought that they were right to teach this, for indeed God did say, Love thy neighbour! But the Pharisees mistakenly extrapolated from this, that God was declaring hatred for an enemy to be righteous, when in fact God's intention was that by this commandment people would learn that they are inherently unjust at heart.

God added the Mosaic Law to the Old Testament in order to convince people of their unrighteousness, with the intent of humbling them so that they may deeply and unreservedly accept Christ's gospel concerning His eternal kingdom. Lev 19:18; Rom 10:1-2; Gal 3:19 & 24-25.

But to you who have already accepted His gospel, Christ - the mediator of the New Testament to God's will - says that you are to bear kindness and consideration towards your enemies as well as your friends, so that you may be a child of God, thoroughly conformed to His Image - thoroughly conformed to Christ. For God is good to all people irrespective of whether they are self-centered [evil] or gracious [good], in that He supplies for everyone the basic requirements to produce nourishment i.e. the sun and the rain. Gal 3:24-25; Heb 9:15; Matt 5:44-45; Rom 8:29.

46-47 For if ye love them which love you, what reward have ye? do not even the publicans the same? And if ye salute your brethren only, what do ye more than others? do not even the publicans so?

For if you bear kindness and consideration - love - only towards those who bear kindness and consideration towards you, and respect only those of the same belief as yourself, then you do no more to glorify God than those who are self-centered [evil] and partial [unjust].

> *48 Be ye therefore perfect even as your Father which is in heaven is perfect.*

Therefore nurture your new spiritual life to maturity [completeness / perfection], capable of teaching others the Truth - that God's subjects <u>must</u> bear kindness and consideration towards all people irrespective of persons, as per Christ's teaching. For only those people who are impartial [complete / perfect] at heart are thoroughly conformed to God's Image, Christ, God's Word incarnate - the New Testament to God's will. Gen 17:1; 2 Tim 3:17; Heb 13:21; Jas 1:4; 2:22; 3:2; Col 2:10; Rom 8:29; Jn 15:17.

As obedient children, not fashioning yourselves according to your former lusts in your ignorance. But as He who has called you is holy, so be you holy - impartial - in all manner of interaction with others. Because it is written, Be you holy, for I am holy. Follow peace with all men, and holiness, without which no one shall see the Lord. For if you have respect of persons - partiality - you commit sin. 1 Pet 1:14-17; Heb 12:14; Jas 2:9.

The scribes and Pharisees believed and taught that God's will is that only certain people are to be reconciled to Him, when in fact God's will is that all people are to be reconciled to Him. Therefore Christ says that people must be reconcilers in order to be endowed with God's favour [Blessed]. 1 Tim 2:4; 2 Cor 5:18-19.

Summary

We must consistently comply with Christ's commands, in order to be righteous - right in life. Rom 7:4-6; Jn 15:4-6; 1 Jn 3:7.

Chapter Four

OUR GOODNESS AT HEART

Holiness

Matthew 6:1-34; 7:1-12.

Having just explained our daily righteousness, Christ then proceeded to explain that it is of value only if it is the product of a good heart [holiness], saying:

Goodness in Relation to God

> *1-4 Take heed that ye do not your alms before men, to be seen of them: otherwise ye have no reward of your Father which is in heaven. Therefore when thou doest thine alms, do not sound a trumpet before thee, as the hypocrites do in the synagogues and in the streets, that they may have glory of men. Verily I say unto you, They have their reward. But when thou doest alms, let not thy left hand know what thy right hand doeth: That thine alms may be in secret: and thy Father which seeth in secret himself shall reward thee openly.*

Mind that you do not give your charitable donations like the hypocrites, who give in front of people to be seen by them, under the pretence of doing so to be seen by God. Instead, give without considering how much, so as to prevent your unrighteous pride of life - your self-importance - from causing you to solicit respect from people. For if you have people's respect, you have your reward from them. Therefore give in secret, so that only your heavenly Father knows your sacrifice, and thereby ensure a reward from Him.

> *5-8 And when thou prayest, thou shalt not be as the hypocrites are: for they love to pray standing in the synagogues and in the corners of the streets, that they may be seen of men. Verily I say unto you, They have their reward. But thou, when thou prayest, enter into thy closet, and when thou hast shut thy door, pray to thy Father which is in secret; and thy Father which seeth in secret shall reward thee openly. But when ye pray, use not vain repetitions, as the heathen do: for they think that they shall be heard for their much speaking. Be not ye therefore like unto them: for your Father knoweth what things ye have need of, before ye ask him.*

Mind that you do not pray like the hypocrites, who pray in front of people to be seen by them, under the pretence of doing so to be seen by God. Instead, pray in solitude, so as to prevent the unrighteous lust of your eyes - your covetousness - from causing you to covet the attention of people. For if you have people's attention, you have your reward from them. Therefore pray in secret, so that only your heavenly Father knows your sacrifice, and thereby ensure a reward from Him.

Also, do not use vain repetitions saying the same thing again and again during a single prayer, believing like the unrighteous - whose prayers are not heeded - that God will heed you if you practise repetitive prayer. For not only does your heavenly Father always heed your prayers - except when you have partiality in your heart - He already knows what you need before you even ask Him. Repetitive prayer, as opposed to persistent / nagging prayer, is therefore futile, for it is offered in doubt, and God only gives to those who ask in faith. Ps 66:18; Prov 15:29; Jas 1:6-7; Heb 11:6.

Be not rash with your mouth, and let not your heart be hasty to utter anything before God. For God is in heaven, and you are on earth. So let your words be few. Eccles 5:2.

9 After this manner therefore pray ye:

Therefore pray in accordance with the Lord's following teaching, praying always for all Christians, that we may all be able to maintain our sacred duty - our service to God - on this temporary earth, as opposed to selfishly praying just for yourself and those Christians that you know of. Eph 6:18.

Our Father which art in heaven,

As one who is contrite at heart - and has therefore deeply and unreservedly accepted Christ's gospel concerning God's eternal kingdom - call upon God by addressing Him as Our Father who is in heaven. For He is the God of heaven who is the Father of the Truth within us, as opposed to the god of this world, Satan, who is the father of lies. 1 Pet 1:23; 2 Cor 4:4; Jn 8:44.

Hallowed be thy name,

As one who has mourned due to Christ's gospel consuming their previous spiritual belief, affirm that you revere and honour the Lord Jesus Christ. For He is the supreme authority, the God of heaven. Isai 43:11-12; Acts 4:12; Titus 2:13.

10 Thy kingdom come. Thy will be done in earth, as it is in heaven.

As one who has become fully and exclusively submissive at heart to the fundamental truth of Christ's gospel, affirm that you submit to Christ's kingdom coming and His will being done absolutely upon earth, as opposed to Satan's present reign through people who do not fully and exclusively submit to the fundamental truth of Christ's gospel. Rom 10:16; Eph 2:2; 5:5-6; Rev 20:6; 21:1; 2 Pet 1:11.

> *11 Give us this day our daily bread.*

As one who genuinely desires knowledge and understanding concerning God's will, ask God to give us all this day our daily requirement of knowledge concerning His will, by which He works within our hearts via His Spirit of graciousness and truth contained therein, both to will and to do His good pleasure. Jn 1:14 & 17; 6:35; 14:17; 17:17; Philip 1:19; 2:13.

> *12 And forgive us our debts, as we forgive our debtors.*

As one who is supporting and nurturing their new spiritual life's potential to consistently bear forgiveness and compassion [mercy] towards all people irrespective of persons, ask God to forgive us all this day our latest offences, as we forgive all those who repent of having offended us, so that we may thereby abide in God's forgiveness and compassion. Lk 17:3-4; Matt 6:15; Jn 15:10.

> *13 And lead us not into temptation,*

As one who is nurturing their new spiritual life's potential to actually bear kindness and consideration [love] towards all people irrespective of persons, ask God to not let us give in to temptation to live in accordance with what we think or feel is right, as opposed to Christ's teaching. Jas 1:13-14; Prov 3:5; Jer 17:9.

> *but deliver us from evil.*

But instead, as one who is nurturing their new spiritual life to maturity [completeness / perfection], capable of teaching others the Truth, ask God to deliver us all this day from self-centeredness, which is evil. 2 Tim 3:17; Heb 13:21; Col 2:10.

> *For thine is the kingdom, and the power, and the glory, forever. Amen.*

Having asked God to give us all this day our daily requirement of knowledge concerning His will, which contains the understanding thereof, then acknowledge that Christ, God's Word incarnate, is actually the supreme authority concerning God's will, and that our membership in God's eternal kingdom is therefore dependent upon Christ's reign over us. 1 Tim 6:15; Rev 19:16.

Having asked God to forgive us all our daily offences, then acknowledge that Christ, God's Word incarnate, has actually been given all power in heaven and on earth, and therefore Christ alone has the power to forever forgive us our sins. Matt 28:18; Heb 1:1-2; 2:1-3; 5:9; 1 Jn 1:9.

Having asked God to not let us give in to temptation to live in accordance with what we think or feel is right, as opposed to Christ's teaching, then acknowledge that Christ, God's Word incarnate, is actually the righteousness of God, and therefore all the works we do in accordance with Christ's teaching are attributed to Him, to His glory. Rom 1:16-17; 10:3-4; Jn 15:5; Philip 2:13; 3:9.

In brief, pray in the following manner:

Our Father in heaven, hallowed be your name, Lord Jesus Christ. May your kingdom come and your will be done absolutely upon earth. Give us all this day our daily requirement of knowledge concerning your will. And forgive us all this day our latest offences, as we forgive all those who repent of having offended us. And do not let us give in to temptation to live in accordance with what we think or feel is right. But rather, deliver us all this day from our self-centeredness. For the kingdom of God, the power to forgive sin, and all the glory from our good works, are yours, forever, Lord Jesus Christ. Amen

14-15 For if ye forgive men their trespasses, your heavenly Father will also forgive you: But if ye forgive not men their trespasses, neither will your Father forgive your trespasses.

For as long as you, in conformance to Christ's teaching - the New Testament to God's will - forgive all those who repent of their offences against you, God will also forgive you all your ongoing daily offences, your ongoing sins against Him. But if you do not forgive others, then neither will God forgive you. Instead, He will hand you over to the devil and his minions [the tormentors] until you pay the price, atone in full, according to your unjustness. Matt 18:21-35; 1 Cor 5:5.

16-18 Moreover when ye fast, be not, as the hypocrites, of a sad countenance: for they disfigure their faces, that they may appear unto men to fast. Verily I say unto you, They have their reward. But thou, when thou fastest, anoint thine head, and wash thy face; That thou appear not unto men to fast, but unto thy Father which is in secret: and thy Father, which seeth in secret, shall reward thee openly.

Mind that you do not fast like the hypocrites, who fast in front of people to be seen by them, under the pretence of doing so to be seen by God. Instead, mask your suffering, so as to prevent the unrighteous lust of your flesh - your self-indulgence - from causing you to enjoy sympathy from people. For if you have people's sympathy, you have your reward from them.

Therefore fast in secret, so that only your heavenly Father knows your sacrifice, and thereby ensure a reward from Him.

Goodness in Relation to Possessions

> *19-21 Lay not up for yourselves treasures upon earth, where moth and rust doth corrupt, and where thieves break through and steal: But lay up for yourselves treasures in heaven, where neither moth nor rust doth corrupt, and where thieves do not break through nor steal: For where your treasure is, there will your heart be also.*

Do not lay up for yourself gain on this temporary earth, only to have it perish, stolen, or inherited by other people. For your future life does not rest in the abundance of the things you possess. It rests in the abundance of the works that you do in accordance with Christ's teaching - the fruit you bear due to God's Spirit of graciousness dwelling within you. You brought nothing into this world, and it is certain that you can carry nothing out. The reward that you get for the works you do now in accordance with Christ's teaching, is the only wealth that you will have in heaven. Lk 12:15; 1 Tim 6:7 & 18-19; Matt 16:27.

Instead of coveting earthly gain, be content with what you need, and sell whatever else you own, and then give what excess money you have to others who need it, so as to lay up spiritual wealth for yourself in heaven to enjoy forever. For wherever you store your wealth, that is where you will hope to enjoy it. Hence if you store up gain in heaven, then your desire will be for heaven, whereas if you store up gain on earth, then your desire will be for the world. Mk 10:21.

Love not the world, nor the things that are in the world. If anyone loves the world, the love of the Father is not in them.

For all that is in the world - the lust of the flesh which is self-indulgence, the lust of the eyes which is covetousness, and the pride of life which is self-importance - is not of the Father, but is of the world. And the world will pass away, and the lust thereof. But whoever does God's will - Christ's teaching - will abide forever. Jas 4:4; 1 Jn 2:15-17; 3:23.

> *22-23 The light of the body is the eye: if therefore thine eye be single, thy whole body shall be full of light. But if thine eye be evil, thy whole body shall be full of darkness. If therefore the light that is in thee be darkness, how great is that darkness!*

The eye is the window through which enlightenment enters the soul. If therefore your eye is single, in that you exclusively regard Christ's teaching - the New Testament to God's will - then you will be full of knowledge and subsequently understanding [light] concerning God's will. But if your eye is self-centered, in that you regard what you think or feel is right, then you will be full of ignorance or misunderstanding [darkness] concerning God's will. Eph 1:17-18.

If therefore the knowledge or understanding that is in you is actually ignorance or misunderstanding concerning God's will, then that ignorance or misunderstanding is very great indeed. For ignorance or misunderstanding due to self-centeredness is actually self-delusion. Eph 4:18.

> *24 No man can serve two masters: for either he will hate the one, and love the other; or else he will hold to the one, and despise the other. Ye cannot serve God and mammon.*

No one can effectively serve two masters. You cannot be faithful to both God and the things of the world. You cannot truly be both godly [benevolent] and worldly [self-indulgent, covetous, and self-important]. For godliness and worldliness are contrary to one another. Gal 5:17.

Therefore have deep and unreserved conviction for Christ's teaching, setting it apart in your mind and heart as complete, so that you may be honest in mind and gracious at heart, and thereby thoroughly conformed to Christ, God's Word incarnate - the New Testament to God's will - full of grace and truth. Lk 8:15; Jn 1:14.

You adulterers and adulteresses, do you not know that the friendship of the world is enmity with God? Whoever therefore will be a friend of the world is the enemy of God. Jas 4:4.

25-33 Therefore I say unto you, Take no thought for your life, what ye shall eat, or what ye shall drink; nor yet for your body, what ye shall put on. Is not the life more than meat, and the body than raiment? Behold the fowls of the air: for they sow not, neither do they reap, nor gather into barns; yet your heavenly Father feedeth them. Are ye not much better than they? Which of you by taking thought can add one cubit unto his stature? And why take ye thought for raiment? Consider the lilies of the field, how they grow; they toil not, neither do they spin: And yet I say unto you, That even Solomon in all his glory was not arrayed like one of these. Wherefore, if God so clothe the grass of the field, which to day is, and to morrow is cast into the oven, shall he not much more clothe you, O ye of little faith? Therefore take no thought, saying, What shall we eat? or, What shall we drink? or, Wherewithal shall we be clothed? (For after all these things do the Gentiles seek:) for your heavenly Father knows that ye have need of all these things. But seek ye first the kingdom of God, and his righteousness; and all these things shall be added unto you.

Since people cannot effectively serve both God and the world, Christ says not to be concerned about your physical life, about having sufficient physical food, drink and clothing. Instead, be concerned about your spiritual life, about having sufficient spiritual food, drink, and clothing, namely, knowledge, understanding, and the robe of righteousness. Prioritise striving to have the eternal things that God wants you to have, instead of the physical things you need. And God will give you both. For God gives eternal things only to those who through deep and unreserved conviction, persistently pray for them, and diligently search for them in His Word. Those who doubt God, receive nothing from God. Isai 61:10; Philip 3:9; Rom 13:14; Col 2:10; Heb 11:6; Lk 16:16; Jas 1:6-8.

> *34 Take therefore no thought for the morrow: for the morrow shall take thought for the things of itself. Sufficient unto the day is the evil thereof.*

Therefore, do not be concerned about the days ahead, about having sufficient physical things. For what will happen in the days ahead, concerns the future. You have enough to be concerned about in the present, with ensuring that you have sufficient knowledge, understanding and righteousness to deliver you from today's self-centeredness, and thereby keep you in fellowship with God, and on the path to His presence in His eternal kingdom. Isai 61:10; Philip 3:9.

Goodness in Relation to People

> *1-2 Judge not, that ye be not judged. For with what judgment ye judge, ye shall be judged: and with what measure ye mete, it shall be measured to you again.*

Do not be judgmental of a fellow human being, so that God

does not likewise condemn you. For those who are unmerciful to other people will receive no mercy from God. Lk 6:37; Jn 7:24.

Therefore, do not be judgmental of non-Christians. For who are you to condemn them? The disciple is not above his master, and our Master - Christ - came to save the world, not to condemn it. Instead, be merciful and loving towards all people as God is merciful and loving towards them i.e. without partiality. Do not condemn non-Christians for their condemnatory words or harmful actions. Instead, be innocent of wrongdoing and of offensive words towards them, so as to be seen by comparison to reprove their unrighteous deeds, in accordance with God's will. For if, in opposition to God's will, you condemn non-Christians, who are full of ignorance or misunderstanding concerning God's will, evidently you yourself are still full of ignorance or misunderstanding [darkness] concerning God's will, and therefore unable to enlighten others. Jn 3:17; Lk 6:31-38; Philip 2:15; Eph 4:18.

Therefore, walk as a child of the light, of true enlightenment, fulfilling the royal law according to the scripture, Thou shalt love thy neighbour as thyself i.e. all those around you at any given time, irrespective of persons. For if you bear kindness and consideration [love] only towards those who bear kindness and consideration towards you, and have respect only for those of the same belief as yourself, you commit sin, and therefore stand convinced by the Mosaic Law as a transgressor of that Law. Eph 5:8; Lk 10:29-37; Jas 2:9-13.

Moreover, do not be judgmental of Christians. For who are you to condemn another man's servant? To his own master he stands or falls, and every true servant of Christ shall be held up, for Christ is able to make him stand. Instead, be fully persuaded in your own mind as to what is lawful under Christ's authority. For every true Christian will stand before the judgment seat of Christ and give account of themselves to Him. Do not condemn other Christians for such things as their regard or disregard for religious ceremony, including what days or foods are holy. For whoever condemns a Christian speaks with self-centeredness [evil] against them, and therefore defies and thereby condemns the law of Christ, which demands graciousness [goodness]. And whoever condemns Christ's law is not a doer of that law, but a condemner, and therefore faces being condemned without mercy. Rom 14:1-6 & 10-12; Gal 6:2; Jas 2:12-13; 4:11-12.

Also, take care not to do anything before a fellow Christian that you understand from Christ's teaching to be lawful under Christ's authority, when they believe it to be unlawful. To do so may cause them to make a mistake by copying you, or to be offended, or to be weakened in faith. For if they believe it to be unlawful, then in effect to them it is sin. Rather, if you are fully persuaded in your own mind from Christ's teaching, that something which other Christians believe to be sin is actually lawful under Christ's authority, then exercise your liberty from the authority of the Mosaic Law, by doing that thing in private, before God only. Rom 14:13-16; 21-23; 1 Cor 8:9-13; 10:23-33.

> *3-5 And why beholdest thou the mote that is in thy brother's eye, but considerest not the beam that is in thine own eye? Or how wilt thou say to thy brother, Let me pull out the mote out of thine eye; and, behold, a beam is in thine own eye? Thou hypocrite, first cast out the beam out of thine own eye; and then shalt thou see clearly to cast out the mote out of thy brother's eye.*

Furthermore, do not even contemplate correcting a fellow Christian's error concerning such things as their regard or disregard for religious ceremony, without first considering your condemnatory attitude towards them, which actually constitutes a greater error and therefore a greater unrighteousness than theirs. For whoever condemns a fellow Christian is not a doer of the law of liberty - the Law of Christ that sets us free from the Law of Moses - but a condemner. Gal 5:18; 6:2; Rom 8:2; Jas 4:11.

Therefore do not attempt to correct a fellow Christian's error concerning such things as religious ceremony, while a condemnatory attitude remains within you. For to do so is hypocrisy. Instead, first remove this greater error from yourself. For only then will you be righteous, as Christ is righteous, and therefore apt to teach, in meekness instructing those who in effect oppose their own conformance to the Image of God, Christ, God's Word incarnate - the New Testament to God's will. 1 Jn 3:7; 2 Tim 2:22-26.

For a good man out of the good treasure of his heart brings forth good things, and an evil man out of the evil treasure of his heart brings forth evil things. In other words, a gracious person out of the Spirit of graciousness and truth - the essence of Christ's teaching - within their heart, brings forth graciousness and truth, and is therefore apt to teach God's will, whereas a self-centered person out of the feelings or opinions within them, brings forth partiality or falsity, and is therefore unable to teach God's will. Matt 12:35; Lk 6:45; Jn 1:14; 14:17; 17:17; Heb 10:29.

> *6 Give not that which is holy unto the dogs, neither cast ye your pearls before swine, lest they trample them under their feet, and turn again and rend you.*

Although our sacred duty on this temporary earth is to glorify God by consistently producing a testament to His will before all those around us irrespective of persons, we are not to be irresponsible in doing so, in case we provoke a hostile response, which would be counter-productive.

Therefore do not persist in producing a testimony to God's will towards those who return to their opinion concerning truth, in case they tear strips off you, and in doing so ruin your testimony to others. 2 Pet 2:22.

Also, do not persist in producing an example of God's will

towards those who return to wallowing in unrighteousness, in case they treat you with contempt, and in doing so ruin your example to others. 2 Pet 2:22.

Be responsible in your sacred duty on this temporary earth, and prevent the unrighteous lust of your eyes - your covetousness - from causing you to covet attention at the expense of your testimony or example.

> *7-11 Ask, and it shall be given you; seek, and ye shall find; knock, and it shall be opened unto you: For every one that asketh receiveth; and he that seeketh findeth; and to him that knocketh it shall be opened. Or what man is there of you, whom if his son ask bread, will he give him a stone? Or if he ask a fish, will he give him a serpent? If ye then, being evil, know how to give good gifts unto your children, how much more shall your Father which is in heaven give good things [the Holy Spirit (Lk 11:13)] to them that ask him?*

In order to consistently produce a testament to God's will before all those around you irrespective of persons, you must be filled continually with knowledge and subsequently understanding concerning God's will specifically from Christ's teaching. For in Christ dwells the fullness of the Godhead incarnate - the Way to God's presence, the Truth from God, and the Life of fellowship with God - and you are complete [whole / perfect] in Him. Col 1:9-10; 2:9-10; Jn 14:6.

Therefore persistently ask God for wisdom concerning His will, that is, plead with God to give you the ability to gain and utilize the knowledge and understanding concerning His will specifically from Christ's teaching. For wisdom concerning God's will is the Way to God's presence. Eph 1:17-18.

Then diligently seek the knowledge concerning God's will specifically from Christ's teaching, that is, study the New

Testament. For the knowledge specifically from Christ's teaching - the New Testament to God's will - is the Truth from God. Heb 1:1-2; 2:1-3; 5:9; 9:15; 2 Cor 3:3-9; Jn 14:6.

Then patiently knock the door to understanding God's will, that is, ponder the Truth you find in Christ's teaching throughout the New Testament, until He opens Himself up to you. For Christ, God's Word incarnate, is the Truth from God, the Door to understanding God's will, by which is the Life of fellowship with God. Jn 10:9; 14:6; Heb 9:15; 2 Tim 2:7.

But mind when asking God for wisdom concerning His will, that you do so believing deeply and unreservedly that He gives it to all abundantly and without rebuke, as the New Testament to His will states. For without faith in God's Word apart from the Mosaic Law, it is impossible to please God. For whoever comes to God must believe that He is, and that He rewards those who diligently seek Him via His Word apart from the Mosaic Law. Jas 1:5-8; 4:8; Heb 11:6; Lk 16:16.

People who directly ask God for wisdom concerning His will, while doubting that He will directly give it to them, they are inconsistent and therefore uncertain in all their ways. They profess that they believe in Christ, and yet they live more in accordance with what they think or feel is right, than they do in accordance with Christ's teaching. They are uncertain in all their ways concerning God's will because they lack the depth or unreservedness of conviction for Christ, required for them to deeply and unreservedly regard His teaching. Jas 1:8; Titus 1:16; 2 Tim 2:15.

Conversely, people who persistently ask God for wisdom i.e. the ability to gain and utilize the knowledge and understanding concerning His will specifically from Christ's teaching, while believing deeply and unreservedly that God will give it to them, they will receive it. Hence those who then diligently seek the knowledge concerning God's will specifically from Christ's teaching, will find it. And those who then patiently ponder the Truth that they find in Christ's teaching throughout the New Testament, will have the door to understanding opened for them.

For since we, who are inherently self-centered, would not refuse any of our biological children's daily request for bread, a fish, or an egg, if those children's physical lives depended on it, then surely God, who is inherently gracious, will not refuse any of His spiritual children's daily request for wisdom, knowledge, and understanding, upon which our spiritual lives depend. Col 1:9; Lk 11:5-13.

> *12 Therefore all things whatsoever ye would that men should do to you, do ye even so to them: for this is the law and the prophets.*

Therefore treat all people as you would have them treat you, as per Christ's teaching, and teach others to do likewise, as He did, so that you may be conformed to Him, God's Son, and thereby deemed one of God's spiritual children - whom God will surely not refuse wisdom, knowledge, and understanding, upon which your new spiritual life depends. Matt 5:44-45; Rom 8:13-14.

For by treating all people as you would have them treat you - not as they actually do treat you - and by teaching others to do likewise, you directly comply with God's will for your daily life, and also indirectly fulfil the Mosaic Law. For Christ, God's Word incarnate, is both the New Testament to God's will and also the fulfilment of the Old. 1 Jn 3:23; Lk 22:20; Heb 9:15; Rom 8:3-4; 10:4; 13:10.

Whatever we ask, we receive from God because we keep His commandments, and do those things that are pleasing in His sight i.e. teach others to do likewise. And this is God's commandment, via the New Testament to His will, That we should believe on the name of His Son Jesus Christ, and love one another, as Christ gave us commandment i.e. trust and obey Christ. 1 Jn 3:22-23.

Owe no one any form of payback, except to love one another as Christ commands. For kindness and consideration works no harm to a fellow human being. Therefore kindness and consideration [love] is the fulfilling of the Mosaic Law. Christ, God's Word incarnate - the New Testament to God's will - is the end of the Mosaic Law concerning God's will. Rom 8:4; 10:4; 13:8-10.

Summary

We must be filled continually with the knowledge and understanding concerning God's will specifically from Christ's teaching, in order to be holy - good at heart. Rom 8:13; 1 Jn 2:16; Rom 12:1-2.

Chapter Five

OUR RIGHTNESS IN GOD'S SIGHT
Justification

Matthew 7:13-28.

Having just explained that our daily righteousness is of value only if it is the product of a good heart [holiness], Christ then proceeded to explain that our faith in Him is valid only if we are faithful to Him, saying:

Rightness Concerning Man's Teaching

> *13-14 Enter ye in at the strait gate: for wide is the gate, and broad is the way, that leadeth to destruction, and many there be which go in thereat: Because strait is the gate, and narrow is the way, which leadeth unto life, and few there be that find it.*

Study and ponder [seek and knock] the teaching from Christ, the strict door to fellowship with God. For the teaching from man is slack, in that it does not demand obedience in regard to behaviour, and the wisdom of man is tolerant of different beliefs, whereas the teaching from Christ is strict, in that it does demand obedience in regard to behaviour, and the wisdom of God is intolerant of different beliefs. Hence many people follow man's teaching, which leads to eternal spiritual death in the lake of fire, and few people actually follow Christ's specific teaching, which leads to eternal spiritual life in God's presence. Prov 14:12; Heb 5:9; Jn 14:6.

Therefore persistently ask God for wisdom concerning His will specifically from Christ's teaching. For it is the Way to His presence. Then diligently seek the knowledge concerning God's will specifically from Christ's teaching. For it is the Truth from God. Then patiently ponder the Truth you find specifically in Christ's teaching. For it is the door to understanding God's will, by which is the Life of fellowship with God. Matt 7:7; Jn 10:9; 14:6.

> *15-20 Beware of false prophets, which come to you in sheep's clothing, but inwardly they are ravening wolves. Ye shall know them by their fruits. Do men gather grapes of thorns, or figs of thistles? Even so every good tree bringeth forth good fruit; but a corrupt tree bringeth forth evil fruit. A good tree cannot bring forth evil fruit, neither can a corrupt tree bring forth good fruit. Every tree that bringeth not forth good fruit is hewn down, and cast into the fire. Wherefore by their fruits ye shall know them.*

Beware of false Christian teachers, who outwardly appear to be members of Christ's flock, but who are actually intent on having people convert to their partially true teaching, and therefore wittingly or unwittingly lead people away from Christ's teaching, which is the Truth from God. You can recognise false Christian teachers by their works. For false Christian teachers bear partial love, whereas true Christian teachers bear impartial love. Indeed, false Christian teachers cannot bear impartial love, because they are not gracious at heart. Therefore, instead of bearing kindness and consideration [love] for all those around them irrespective of persons, as per Christ's teaching, false Christian teachers naturally bear kindness and consideration only for those who bear kindness and consideration for them, and they naturally show respect only for those of the same belief as themselves. Lk 6:45; Matt 5:46-47.

The teaching from man is that people are regarded as right

[justified] in God's sight through compliance with the Mosaic Law - primarily the Ten Commandments. Yet God's Word apart from the Mosaic Law clearly states that no flesh will be justified in His sight by the deeds of the Mosaic Law. People are actually justified in God's sight by living in accordance with their faith in His Word apart from the Mosaic Law. Rom 3:20-24; 9:32; Philip 3:9; Gal 2:16; Jas 2:21-22; Heb 11:8.

That is not to say that the Mosaic Law is not in accordance with God's will i.e. that it is unrighteous. For the purpose of the Mosaic Law is to convince people of their unrighteousness, their sin, in order to humble them so that they may deeply and unreservedly accept Christ's gospel concerning God's eternal kingdom. The Mosaic Law defines unrighteousness [sin] in order to teach people why they do unrighteousness, and it is in accordance with God's will i.e. righteous, in doing so. Rom 3:19-20; 7:7; 1 Tim 1:8.

God does not impute righteousness to people for directly keeping the Mosaic Law, because that Law is not intended to define righteousness. It is actually intended to define unrighteousness - adultery, theft, bearing false witness, etc. God imputes righteousness to those who live in accordance with their faith in His Word apart from the Mosaic Law. For God's Word apart from the Mosaic Law clearly defines righteousness - longsuffering, gentleness, goodness, etc. God added the Mosaic Law to the Old Testament in order to convince people of their unrighteousness [sin], with the intent of humbling them so that they may deeply and unreservedly accept His Word apart from the Mosaic Law. Exod 20:14-16; Gal 2:21; 3:19; 5:19-25; Jn 1:14.

Hence God has in the New Testament to His will clarified what has always been the Truth from Him, that the just shall live by faith, that is, that those who are regarded as right in God's sight will have spiritual life in accordance with their faith in His Word apart from the Mosaic Law. But if anyone draws back from God's Word apart from the Mosaic Law, God's soul shall have no pleasure in that person. They draw back to spiritual death and ultimately eternal punishment in the lake of fire. They do not believe to the saving of their soul. They fall from grace, from the Spirit of God's graciousness contained within His Word apart from the Mosaic Law. Rom 1:16-17; Heb 10:38-39; Gal 5:4-6.

The teaching that people should directly keep the Mosaic Law, even in principle, is therefore another gospel than that from Christ. It is not a completely different gospel, but a distorted version of Christ's gospel. For those who consistently comply with Christ's commands actually, yet indirectly, fulfil the Mosaic Law. Just as a person who obeys a command to stand, indirectly fulfils another command not to sit, so likewise those who comply with Christ's commands to love one another, indirectly fulfil the Mosaic Law's commandments not to bear false witness against one another, etc. By faithfully living in accordance with the all-encompassing essence of Christ's teaching, true Christians actually yet indirectly keep the limited letter of the Mosaic Law, whereas those who attempt to directly keep the Mosaic Law, even in principle, actually fail to fulfil the righteousness of it i.e. the bearing of impartial love, as commanded by Christ. The teaching that Christians should directly keep the Mosaic Law, even in principle, can be perceived as synonymous with Christ's teaching, but it is not. It is actually a distorted version of Christ's gospel. Gal 1:6-7; 3:1-7; Rom 9:31-33; 13:10; Jn 15:17.

Indeed, any conviction a Christian may have to directly keep the Mosaic Law, even in principle, is actually unfaithfulness to Christ. For having put their faith in Christ as the end of the Mosaic Law concerning righteousness, true Christians have been freed from the authority of the Mosaic Law through association with Christ's death, and spiritually reborn through association with Christ's resurrection, so that they may be espoused to Christ and therefore subject to His authority without committing spiritual adultery against the Mosaic Law [their former husband]. Hence any Christian who intentionally returns to directly keeping the Mosaic Law, even in principle, effectively commits spiritual adultery against Christ. Rom 6:3-

14; Col 2:12-14; Rom 7:1-4; 2 Cor 11:2.

You have been liberated from the authority of the Mosaic Law so that you may be free to serve God in accordance with the all-encompassing Spirit of graciousness contained within Christ's teaching, and thereby bear the fruit thereof to God's glory. But if you intentionally return to directly keeping the Mosaic Law, even in principle, you would in effect put yourself back under its authority. You would therefore no longer be under Christ's authority - His commands to love others in accordance with the Spirit of graciousness. You would fall from grace, from the all-encompassing Spirit of graciousness contained within Christ's teaching. Hence you would no longer face being judged according to how gracious you have been. Instead, you would be judged according to how well you have kept the Mosaic Law. And no one will be justified in God's sight by the works of the Mosaic Law. Rom 7:4-6; Heb 10:29; Gal 2:21; 5:1-9; Rom 2:12; 3:20 & 24; Jas 2:12.

Beloved, seeing you know these things, beware lest you also, being led away with the error of the wicked, fall from your own steadfastness i.e. fall from grace. But grow in graciousness, and in the knowledge of our Lord and Saviour Jesus Christ. To Him be glory both now and forever. Amen. 2 Pet 3:17-18.

Let us declare the Word of God apart from the Mosaic Law, instantly in and out of season. Let us reprimand, sharply criticise, and strongly urge, with patience and with Christ's teaching. For the time will come when people will not endure sound doctrine, the teaching from Christ. Instead, after their own lusts they will heap to themselves false teachers to appease their desire for pleasing words. They will turn their ears away from the Truth. And they will be turned to false beliefs. 2 Tim 4:2-4; Titus 1:9-14.

There will be false teachers among us, who will covertly bring in beliefs contrary to Christ's teaching i.e. damnable heresies, even denying the Lord that bought them with His own blood, by disregarding His teaching. Many people will follow their destructive ways, and because of them the teaching from Christ - the Truth - will be discussed with self-centeredness. Moreover, with false teaching they will cause Christians to covet the attention of others, and thereby use such Christians to promote their erroneous beliefs. 2 Pet 2:1-3; Titus 1:16.

The final days leading up to Christ's return to physically establish His eternal kingdom, initially on this temporary earth, will be especially dangerous and risky times for faithful Christians. For in the final days leading up to Christ's return, faithful Christians will face constant danger of spiritual corruption due to false teaching.

For Christian leaders in general will be spiritually corrupt, and therefore lovers of themselves, in that they will revere and honour themselves more than they do Christ. They will be covetous, in that they will desire the attention of others. They will be boasters, in that they will talk with excessive pride and self-satisfaction. And they will be proud, in that they will have an excessively high opinion of themselves. They will be blasphemers, in that they will speak vainly about God. They will be disobedient to parents, in that they will disregard parent's authority. And they will be unthankful, in that they will show no sincere appreciation for the sacrifice of others. They will be unholy, in that they will have partiality in their heart. They will be without natural affection, in that they will show no fondness for people in general. And they will be truce breakers, in that they will not be appeased. They will be false accusers, in that they will rebut criticism with accusation. They will be incontinent, in that they will lack control over their partiality. And they will be fierce, in that they will show a fierce loyalty to their beliefs. They will be despisers of those who are good, in that they will have contempt for those who are genuinely gracious at heart. They will be traitors, in that they will be unfaithful to Christ, God's Word incarnate - the New Testament to God's will. And they will be heady, in that they will have an exhilarating effect. They will be high-minded, in that they will have strong moral principles, and will therefore strongly advocate "the moral law". They will be lovers of pleasures more than lovers of God, in that they will desire the feeling of happy satisfaction more than the Truth. And they will have a form of godliness, but deny the power thereof, in that they will appear to be benevolent, to God's glory, but they will actually deny God that glory, by their hypocrisy. From such people turn away. 2 Tim 3:1-5.

For they are the sort of people who gradually charm their way into houses, and proselytise women who are easy prey, women who are less wise than others and burdened with sin. They lead people away from Christ's teaching with a diversity of worldly desires, people who are ever learning, and yet never able to come to the knowledge of the Truth concerning God's will. 2 Tim 3:6-7.

Just as Jannes and Jambres, by means of counterfeit signs and wonders, withstood Moses i.e. what he said concerning God's will, which God validated with real signs and wonders, so do false Christian teachers, by means of counterfeit signs and wonders, resist the Truth i.e. what Christ said concerning God's will, which God validated with real signs and wonders. They are people of corrupt minds, reprobate, having no principles - no fundamental truth / foundation - concerning the faith. Their testament to God's will [house / plant] is not built upon the fact that all people must now be reconciled to God by faith in Christ as the sacrificial Lamb, and regarded as right in God's sight by faithfulness to Christ as the resurrected Lord. 2 Tim 3:8. Exod 7:3 & 10-11; Heb 2:3-4; Matt 24:24.

Beware of the erroneous teaching [opinions] of man, so as to avoid the risk of falling away from Christ's gospel concerning God's eternal kingdom, and thereby falling from graciousness. Persistently pray for the wisdom of God, and study and ponder the teaching from Christ, which is the strict door to fellowship with God, to ensure that you have fellowship with God and are on the path to His presence in His eternal kingdom.

If anyone teaches otherwise, and consents not to wholesome words, the words of our Lord Jesus Christ, the teaching that is according to godliness - that God's subjects <u>must</u> bear kindness and consideration towards all people irrespective of persons - they are proud, knowing nothing, but doting about questions and disagreements of words, which causes envy, disagreement, denouncing, evil conjecture, and perverse arguments of people of corrupt minds. These people are destitute of the Truth, supposing that gain is godliness. From such people withdraw yourself. 1 Tim 6:3-5.

Metaphorically speaking: Man's opinion is the essence of Stony Ground. Therefore whoever keeps man's teaching in their heart is Stony Ground.

Rightness Concerning Christ's Teaching

21 Not every one that saith unto me, Lord, Lord, shall enter into the kingdom of heaven; but he that doeth the will of my Father which is in heaven [...the things which I say (Lk 6:46)].

Christ insists that not everyone who emphatically calls Him Lord will actually inherit God's eternal kingdom. It is people who do God's will, that is, who believe in Christ and consequently live in accordance with His teaching, that will actually inherit God's eternal kingdom. 1 Jn 3:23; Jas 1:22; 2 Pet 1:11; Heb 5:9.

The teaching from Christ is that people are regarded as right in God's sight through living in accordance with their faith in God's Word apart from the Mosaic Law. For the righteousness that is by faith says: That if you will confess with your mouth the Lord Jesus - God's Word incarnate - and will believe in your heart that God has raised Him from the dead, you will be saved. For with the heart, man believes to righteousness i.e. to doing God's will, and with the mouth, confession is made to salvation i.e. to the salvation of the person making the confession and of those who hear it. Hence whoever by faith in Christ - God's Word incarnate - consistently complies with His commands, and teaches others to do likewise, they are justified in God's sight by faith in God's Word apart from the Mosaic Law. Confession is a confession of faith that sets out the fundamental truth of Christ's teaching, the essential doctrine of Christianity - that God's subjects must bear kindness and consideration [love] towards all people irrespective of persons. Rom 10:9-12; Heb 1:1-2; 2:1-3; 1 Tim 4:16; 1 Jn 3:23; Jn 15:10-17; Philip 3:9; Lk 16:16; Rom 3:28; Jas 2:20-24; Heb 5:9.

People are not regarded as right [justified] in God's sight without works, by faith itself, alone. For faith without works is unproductive - dead / barren of good fruit - in that it produces no testament to God's will, to His glory. People are regarded as right in God's sight by their depth and unreservedness of conviction for His Word apart from the Mosaic Law causing them to do His will apart from the Mosaic Law. Faith in God's Word incarnate [Christ] is invalid without faithfulness to that Word [Christ's teaching]. Jas 2:17-24; Heb 11:8; Jas 1:21-22.

You are justified in God's sight by grace, because it is God's Spirit of graciousness that works in your heart to do God's will. And you are justified in God's sight by faith, because it is your faith in Christ - God's Word incarnate - that causes you to live in accordance with His Spirit of graciousness working in your heart to do God's will. Rom 3:24; Philip 2:13; Heb 10:29; Rom 5:1; Gal 3:11; Philip 3:9; Rom 8:13-14.

For by grace - God's Spirit of graciousness dwelling within you - are you saved, through faith in Christ. And it is not of yourselves. It - the Spirit of graciousness - is the gift of God. You are not saved by works pertaining to the flesh, lest any man [flesh] should boast. For we are God's workmanship, created in Christ Jesus to do good works pertaining to God's Spirit of graciousness working in our hearts to do righteousness, which God has before ordained that we should walk in. And we do good works only because God works in us, via His Spirit of graciousness contained with His Word apart from the Mosaic Law, both to will and to do His good pleasure. Eph 2:8-10; 3:7; Heb 10:29; Philip 2:13; Jn 1:14.

What shall we say then that Abraham our father, as <u>pertaining to the flesh</u>, has found? For if Abraham were justified by works <u>pertaining to the flesh</u>, he has that to glory i.e. glory by works pertaining to the flesh. But not before God. Abraham's glory would be before other people - other flesh. For what does scripture say? Abraham believed God - and therefore lived in accordance with his faith in God's word apart from the Mosaic Law - and it was counted to him for righteousness, compliance with God's will. Rom 4:1-3; Jas 2:21.

Now to those who do works pertaining to the flesh, the reward is not calculated according to how gracious they have been. It is calculated according to how well they have kept the Mosaic Law. But to those who do not do works pertaining to the flesh, but instead believe on Him that justifies self-centered people [the ungodly] by the free gift of His Spirit of graciousness dwelling in their hearts, their faith is counted as compliance with God's will. Rom 4:4-5; Gal 5:1-3; Eph 2:8.

What does it profit, my brethren, though a man says that he has faith, and yet he has no works - <u>pertaining to God's Spirit of graciousness</u>? Can faith save him? If a brother or sister needs clothing or food, and one of you say to them that you wish them peace, warmth and a full stomach, and yet you do not give them any clothing or food, what does it profit? Likewise, faith, if it has not works <u>pertaining to God's Spirit of graciousness</u>, is dead, being alone. One person may say to another, You have faith, and I have works. Show me your faith, your trust in God as the supreme authority, without your works, your active submission to that authority. And I will show you my faith, my trust in God as the supreme authority, by my works, my active submission to that authority. You believe that there is one God. You do well. But the demons also believe this, and tremble. For although they believe in and fear God, they do not trust in God as the supreme authority. But will you, O vain person, accept that faith in God as the supreme authority without active submission to His authority is unproductive, and therefore invalid? Jas 2:14-20.

Was not Abraham our forefather justified by works, apart from the Mosaic Law, when he had offered Isaac his son upon the altar? See how faith functioned with his works, and by his works apart from the Mosaic Law his faith was made perfect i.e. complete? And the scripture was fulfilled which says, Abraham believed God - and therefore lived in accordance with his faith in God's word apart from the Mosaic Law - and it was imputed to him as compliance with God's will [righteousness]. And he was called the Friend of God. You see then how that by works, which God has before ordained that we should walk in, a man is justified. And not by faith only. Not by faith alone. For as the body without the spirit of life - which God breathed into Adam - is dead and thus unproductive, so faith without works pertaining to God's Spirit of graciousness is also dead and thus unproductive. Jas 2:21-26; Eph 2:10; Rom 8:1-2.

Where is boasting then? It is excluded. By what law? Of works? No. But by the law of faith. Therefore we conclude that a person is justified through living in accordance with faith in God's Word, without the deeds of the Mosaic Law. Rom 3:27-28.

Do we then make void the Mosaic Law through faith in God's Word apart from the Mosaic Law? God forbid. Actually, we establish the Mosaic Law. For by living in accordance with our faith in Christ, who defines righteousness, we confirm the righteousness of the Mosaic Law in its defining of unrighteousness. Rom 3:31; 7:7; 13:10; Jn 15:17.

Stand fast therefore in the liberty by which Christ, God's Word incarnate - the New Testament to God's will - has made us free, and be not entangled again with the yoke of bondage, the authority of the Mosaic Law. For Christ says that if you continue in His word - His teaching - you are a Christian indeed. And you will know the Truth concerning God's will, and the Truth will make you free from the law of sin and death, the Mosaic Law, which convicts of sin and therefore condemns to spiritual death. Gal 5:1; Jn 8:31-32; Rom 8:1-2.

If you keep Christ's teaching, and teach others to do likewise, as He did, you will be conformed to Him, God's Son, and thereby deemed one of God's spiritual children. Then God will grant you your daily request for wisdom, knowledge, and understanding, upon which your new spiritual life depends. Then you will know the Truth from God - that people are justified in God's sight by their faith in His Word apart from the Mosaic Law causing them to do His will apart from the Mosaic Law. And you will then faithfully submit to Christ as the supreme authority, and thereby be set free from the authority of Mosaic Law. For the Mosaic Law is against the unrighteousness of the flesh, and its authority therefore applies to those who gratify the flesh. But those who faithfully submit to Christ do not gratify their flesh - hatred, wrath, strife, etc. They bear the fruit of God's Spirit - love, longsuffering, gentleness, etc. And there is no law against doing so. Gal 5:16-23.

The Mosaic Law is not made for a righteous person e.g. one who complies with Christ's commands: the Law of Christ. It is made for the lawless and disobedient, for the ungodly, and for sinners. It is for the unholy and irreverent, for murderers of fathers and murderers of mothers, and for manslayers. It is for whoremongers, for them that defile themselves with mankind, and for those who lead people away from Christ. It is for liars, for people who make false oaths, and for people who do any other thing that is contrary to Christ's teaching, sound doctrine. 1 Tim 1:9-10; Gal 6:2.

Let no one deceive you, whoever does righteousness i.e. lives in accordance with Christ's teaching, is righteous, even as Christ is righteous. 1 Jn 3:7.

Stand fast in this freedom from the Mosaic Law. Yet not so as to justify doing as you please, which may be harmful to others. But rather so as to serve others in accordance with God's Spirit of graciousness working in your heart to do His will. Therefore submit yourself to every ordinance of man, whether it be the king, or governors, or them that are sent by governors. For it is God's will that we put to silence the rationalizations of foolish people, who abide by their own principles of right and wrong, rather than by an external authority, a law. It is God's will that we be innocent of wrongdoing and of offensive words, without rebuke in the midst of a crooked and perverse nation, so as to be seen by comparison to reprove their unrighteous deeds. Gal 5:13; 1 Pet 2:12-16; 1 Tim 1:9; Philip 2:15.

Be kind and considerate towards all people irrespective of persons, as per Christ's teaching. For it is by your impartial kindness and consideration [love] that people will see that you are a true Christian, and also that you yourself will know that you have definitely passed from spiritual death to spiritual life. For impartial kindness and consideration is from God. And everyone who is kind and considerate towards all people irrespective of persons, is therefore born of God, and knows God. Jn 13:35; 15:17; 1 Jn 3:14; 4:7-8; 5:13.

Whoever consistently complies with Christ's commands - the New Testament to God's will - dwells in Christ, and has Christ abiding in them. And we know that Christ abides in us, by the Spirit of graciousness that he has given us. For if we have this world's good and see that a fellow human being has need, and yet we show no compassion for that person, by refusing to give them what they need, such as clothing and food, how can the love of God be in us? Therefore do not love people merely in word. Instead, be kind and considerate [loving] towards people, in action and in honesty, in accordance with the Spirit of graciousness that God has given you. 1 Jn 3:24; Jn 15:10; Eph 2:8; 3:7; 1 Jn 3:17-18.

Whoever is born of God cannot wilfully be mean and inconsiderate towards anyone, because God's Spirit of graciousness remains within their heart, condemning their unrighteousness to death in their flesh and working to do righteousness. Any mean or inconsiderate - hating / sinful - deed done by a person born of God is therefore done against their new core spiritual desire i.e. un-wilfully. Therefore it is no longer they that sin. It is their sinful flesh. For during His death and resurrection to life, Christ made it possible for our unrighteousness [sin] to be condemned to death within our physical bodies, our flesh, by the presence of God's Spirit within our spiritual cores, so that our souls may be saved from condemnation. For without God's Spirit of graciousness [divine nature] dwelling within, no one has any genuine goodness. And without genuine goodness, which is holiness, no one will see the Lord. 1 Jn 3:9; 5:17-18; Rom 7:15-25; 8:1-4; Matt 5:17; Heb 12:14.

Whoever does not actually bear kindness and consideration [love] towards all people irrespective of persons, as per Christ's teaching, is not born of God. Likewise, whoever does not sincerely love all true Christians is not born of God. For this is the message that we have heard from the beginning - from God via the Old Testament to His will - that we should love our neighbour as we love ourselves. 1 Jn 3:10-11; 4:7-8; Lev 19:18.

Metaphorically speaking: Any branch engrafted into the vine, that submits to the vine, dwells in the vine, and the vine in it. And we know that the vine abides in the engrafted branch, by the presence of the sap of the vine within it. An engrafted branch that truly takes to the vine cannot wilfully bear its own fruit, because the sap, or nature, of the vine remains within that branch's heart, condemning that branch's badness to death in its body, and working to bear good fruit. Any bad fruit produced by an engrafted branch that truly takes to the vine is therefore done against that branch's new core desire i.e. un-wilfully. Therefore it is no longer the branch that bears bad fruit. It is its body. Any branch engrafted into the vine that does not bear good fruit, has not truly taken to the vine. For the vine always compels the bearing of good fruit. Jn 15:1-10.

If we say that we have fellowship with Christ, God's Word incarnate - the New Testament to God's will - and yet walk in ignorance or misunderstanding [darkness] concerning God's will, we lie, and do not the Truth. But if we walk in the understanding [light] from Christ - that God's subjects <u>must</u> bear kindness and consideration towards all people irrespective of persons - then we have fellowship with all true Christians, and the blood of Christ cleanses us from all unrighteousness. Jn 1:9-12; 1 Jn 1:6-7.

If after you have received the knowledge of the Truth, you say that you no longer have meanness or inconsideration [sin], you deceive yourself, and you misunderstand Christ's teaching concerning God's will. In effect, you sin un-wilfully, and deny it. Hence your ongoing sins are not forgiven. For you are nurturing feelings that are contrary to God's will, as well as Christ's gospel concerning God's eternal kingdom, and are thus depriving your new spiritual life of nourishment. Metaphorically speaking: You are Thorny Ground. 1 Jn 1:8; Jas 4:8-10.

If after you have received the knowledge of the Truth, you confess the meanness and inconsideration [sin] that you still commit due to your flesh, Christ is faithful and just to forgive you, and to cleanse you from all unrighteousness. In effect, you sin un-wilfully, and confess it. Hence your ongoing sins are forgiven. For you are honest in mind, and gracious at heart, and are thus supporting and nurturing your new spiritual life. Metaphorically speaking: You are Good Ground. 1 Jn 1:9; Rom 4:25; 14:9.

If after you have received the knowledge of the Truth, you say that you no longer commit meanness and inconsideration [sin], you make Christ out to be a liar, and you are wilfully ignorant of Christ's teaching concerning God's will. In effect, you sin wilfully, and deny it. Hence there remains no more sacrifice for sins for you. For you are full of opinions concerning God's will, and have therefore abandoned Christ's Gospel concerning God's eternal kingdom. Metaphorically speaking: You are Stony Ground. 1 Jn 1:10; Rom 10:3; Philip 3:9; Heb 10:26; 2 Pet 3:17-18.

Christians who have ignorance or misunderstanding in their hearts concerning God's will, erroneously believe that salvation is a gift from God, that salvation is received upon conversion, and that continued unrighteousness [sin] following professed conversion means either, [1] that salvation has not actually been received, or [2] that salvation will ultimately be lost.

They do not understand that God's Spirit of graciousness is actually the gift from God, that conversion is brought about by God's Spirit of graciousness within a person's heart, and that continued sin following conversion does not necessarily have any bearing on a person's salvation. For God's spirit of graciousness dwelling in a person's heart condemns their unrighteousness to death in their flesh. Hence any unrighteousness [sin] committed following a person's true conversion is done by their flesh against their new core spiritual desire, and therefore not attributed to them personally, as long as they confess any meanness and inconsideration that they still commit. Furthermore, once a person's unrighteousness is truly condemned to death in their flesh by the indwelling of God's Spirit of graciousness, their soul is no longer under the authority of the Mosaic Law and therefore no longer deemed guilty of any transgression of that law, as long as they confess any meanness and inconsideration that they still commit. Eph 2:8; 3:7-8; Heb 10:29; Rom 6:14-18; 7:16-25; 8:1-4; 1 Jn 3:6-11; 5:16-18; 1 Pet 1:22; Rom 4:15.

True conversion is not change to a godly life. It is change to a godly heart. Therefore a person's salvation is not dependent on the quantity of their good works following conversion. It is dependent on the goodness of their heart. For even if a person's good work [rightness in life] is continually destroyed by accusations from the devil, as long as that person has the depth and unreservedness of conviction for Christ to remain at least to some extent consistently compliant with His commands, that person will be saved, whereas without goodness at heart, which is holiness, no one will see the Lord. Lk 8:15; Philip 3:9; Titus 3:5; 1 Cor 3:15; Heb 5:9; 12:14.

The correct understanding concerning salvation is that people are redeemed from their past sins and from the curse of the Mosaic Law, by the shedding of Christ's blood on the cross, and are redeemed from all partiality thereafter, by God's Spirit of graciousness dwelling in their heart. God's Spirit of graciousness is the gift from God, which brings about a person's conversion - change to a godly heart - so that their soul may be rescued from their body of death unto eternal life in a new incorruptible body. This has all been accomplished by Jesus Christ condemning unrighteousness to death within His physical body, by the presence of God's Spirit of graciousness within His spiritual core during His death and resurrection to life. And people are regarded as personally right in God's sight by their faith in God's Word apart from the Mosaic Law, causing them to at least to some extent consistently comply with that Word, in accordance with God's Spirit of graciousness dwelling in their heart. Heb 9:15; Gal 3:13; Titus 2:14; Rom 4:25; 14:8-9; Philip 2:13; Eph 2:8; 3:7-8; Rom 7:24-25; 8:1-4; 1 Pet 1:9; 1 Cor 15:49-53; Rom 3:28; Jas 2:20-24.

Christians who are full of understanding [light] concerning God's will, correctly understand that God's Spirit of graciousness is the gift from God, that the presence of God's Spirit of graciousness within a person's heart actually brings about conversion, and that continued self-centeredness following professed conversion means that Christ's gospel concerning God's eternal kingdom has not been deeply and unreservedly accepted at stage one of spiritual development [See chapter one], and therefore true conversion - change to a godly heart - has not actually occurred. Eph 2:8; Titus 3:5; Rom 8:9-14; 1 Pet 1:22-23.

My little children, these things I write to you so that you do not be mean and inconsiderate towards anyone i.e. sin. And if any of us do sin un-wilfully, we have an advocate with the Father, that is, Jesus Christ the righteous. Christ is the appeasement for our sins. And not for our sin only. But also for the sins of the whole world. And we know that we know Christ by the fact that we at least to some extent consistently comply with His commands. 1 Jn 2:1-3.

Whoever says that they know Christ, and yet does not at least to some extent consistently comply with his commands, is a liar, and the Truth is not in them. But whoever at least to some extent consistently complies with Christ's commands, in them is the love of God perfected i.e. completed. And by God's love being completed in us, we know that we are in Christ. He that says that he abides in Christ ought himself also to live even as Christ lived - bearing kindness and consideration towards all people irrespective of persons, and teaching others to do likewise. 1 Jn 2:4-6.

Brethren, I am not writing a new commandment to you. I am writing an old commandment that you have had from the beginning i.e. love thy neighbour as thyself. The old commandment is the word that you have heard from the beginning via the Old Testament to God's will. And yet it is a new commandment that I am writing to you, in that it is differently defined i.e. love one another as Christ has loved us. This new commandment is true in Christ, and in you as long as Christ's teaching abides in your heart, because the ignorance and misunderstanding concerning God's will is past, and the correct understanding concerning God's will now shines from Christ's teaching, which is the New Testament to God's will. Lev 19:18; 1 Jn 2:7-8; 3:23-24. Jn 13:34; 15:17

Whoever confidently says that they are abiding in understanding concerning God's will, and yet is consistently mean and inconsiderate - hating / sinful - towards a fellow human being, they are actually still abiding in ignorance concerning God's will. Hence they are surely on their way to the lake of fire. They are surely not saved, because they are full of ignorance concerning salvation itself. Metaphorically speaking: They are Stony Ground. 1 Jn 1:10; 2:9.

Whoever is consistently kind and considerate - loving / sinless - towards all their fellow human beings, they are abiding in the understanding from Christ concerning God's will, and there is no ignorance or misunderstanding within them that will cause them to stumble in their sacred duty, their service to God. Hence they can be sure that they are on their way to God's presence in His eternal kingdom. They can be sure of their salvation, because they are full of understanding concerning salvation itself. Metaphorically speaking: They are Good Ground. 1 Jn 1:9; 2:10.

Whoever is consistently mean and inconsiderate - hating / sinful - towards a fellow human being, and does not confidently say that they are abiding in understanding concerning God's will, they are actually abiding in misunderstanding concerning God's will. Hence they are unsure of whether they are on their way to God's presence in His eternal kingdom or on their way to the lake of fire. They are unsure of their salvation because they are full of misunderstanding concerning salvation itself. Metaphorically speaking: They are Thorny Ground. 1 Jn 1:8; 2:11.

Therefore lay apart all filthiness and superfluity of naughtiness. And receive with meekness the engrafted word, Christ, God's Word incarnate - the New Testament to God's will - which is able to save your souls. But be doers of the word, and not only hearers, deceiving your own selves. In other words, set aside all offences and disobedience to God's will, and fully and exclusively submit yourself to the fundamental truth of Christ's gospel, thoroughly fulfilling phases one through to three of spiritual development [see chapter one]. But be sure to also consistently comply with Christ's commands, and teach others to do likewise, fulfilling phases five through to seven, by ensuring that you are actually satisfied [filled] with the knowledge and understanding concerning God's will specifically from Christ's teaching at phase four. For if you believe that your soul is saved, even though you do not at least to some extent consistently comply with Christ's commands, and teach others to do likewise, then you are deceiving yourself, in that you fail to admit to yourself that you do not have either the depth or the unreservedness of conviction for Christ, God's Word incarnate - the New Testament to God's will - required to save your soul. Metaphorically speaking: You are either Stony or Thorny Ground. Jas 1:21-22.

People who are not satisfied with the knowledge and understanding concerning God's will specifically from Christ's teaching at phase four of spiritual development, they are ever learning and yet never able to come to the knowledge of the Truth concerning God's will - that God's subjects must bear kindness and consideration [love] towards all people irrespective of persons, as per Christ's teaching. They are forever consuming scripture, yet never able to retain sufficient knowledge or understanding concerning God's will specifically from Christ's teaching, to be satisfied [filled] with graciousness and truth. They therefore fall away from Christ's gospel, due to opinions at phase five of spiritual development, or they deprive their new spiritual life of nourishment, due to feelings at phase six. Hence they fail in their sacred duty on this temporary earth, by failing to consistently produce a testament to God's will. They are therefore unprofitable servants of God, destined for the lake of fire. For whoever falls away from Christ's gospel abandons Christ. And whoever deprives their new spiritual life of nourishment will be rejected by Christ. 2 Tim 3:7; Heb 2:3; Matt 25:30.

Therefore be sure to go on from the basic principles of Christ's teaching, on to maturity - completeness / perfection - by living in accordance with Christ's teaching to impartially love others. Do not keep laying again and again the basic principles of repentance, faith, baptism, laying on of hands, resurrection, and judgment. Push on to maturity, fulfilling phases five through to seven of spiritual development, by ensuring that you are actually satisfied with the knowledge and understanding concerning God's will specifically from Christ's teaching at phase four. For whoever falls away from Christ's gospel at phase five, cannot go on to phase seven and maturity [completeness / perfection]. Nor can they revert to phase one and repentance. Likewise, whoever deprives their new spiritual life of nourishment at phase six, cannot go on to phase seven and maturity [completeness / perfection], unless they first revert to phase one and repentance. Heb 6:1-3.

For it is impossible for people who were once enlightened, have tasted of the heavenly gift, were made partakers of the Holy Ghost, and have tasted the good word of God, and the powers of the world to come, if they shall fall away, to renew them again to repentance, seeing that they crucify to themselves the Son of God afresh, and put Him to an open shame. In other words, it is impossible for people who have experienced the first four phases of spiritual development [see chapter one], if they then abandon Christ's gospel concerning God's eternal kingdom at phase five, for them to revert to phase one and repentance. For people in abandoning Christ's gospel concerning God's eternal kingdom, make Christ, God's Word incarnate - the New Testament to God's will - unproductive to themselves, and publicly discredit the soundness of His gospel by openly abandoning it. Heb 6:4-6.

Metaphorically speaking: Stony Ground falls away from the farmer's seed because it has not been filled with new rain, whereas Good Ground drinks in the new rain that comes upon it often, and brings forth seed-bearing plants, and is therefore blessed. But Thorny Ground, even though it drinks in the new rain, bears thorns and briers, and is therefore rejected and near to cursing by the farmer. Heb 6:7-8; 12:15.

Let us therefore be mindful of Christ's teaching, and live in accordance with it, being kind and considerate - loving / sinless - towards all our fellow human beings irrespective of persons, and teaching others to do likewise. For by doing so, we will both save ourselves and those that hear us. 1 Tim 4:16; Jn 15:12.

And be not conformed to this world. But be you transformed by the renewing of your mind - brainwashed by the essence of

Christ's teaching, the Spirit of Truth - so that you may prove what is that good, acceptable and perfect i.e. complete, will of God. Rom 12:2; 2 Tim 3:17.

And this is God's commandment, God's will for our daily lives, That we should believe on the name of His Son Jesus Christ, and love one another, as Christ gave us commandment i.e. trust and obey Christ. 1 Jn 3:23.

Whoever transgresses, and does not abide in Christ's teaching, has not God. But whoever abides in Christ's teaching has both the Father and the Son. 2 Jn 1:9.

Hence whoever by faith in Christ, God's Word incarnate - the New Testament to God's will - faithfully lives in accordance with His teaching, and teaches others to do likewise, they are regarded as right [justified] in God's sight by faith in His Word apart from the Mosaic Law. Rom 10:9-11; Philip 3:9.

Metaphorically speaking: God's graciousness and truth is the essence of Good Ground. Therefore whoever keeps Christ's teaching in their heart is Good Ground.

Rightness Concerning the Devil's Teaching

> *22-23 Many will say to me in that day, Lord, Lord, have we not prophesied in thy name? and in thy name have cast out devils? and in thy name done many wonderful works? And then will I profess unto them, I never knew you: depart from me, ye that work iniquity.*

Christ says that when He returns to physically establish His eternal kingdom, initially on this temporary earth, many will emphatically insist that they have served Him as Lord. Yet He will declare to them that He was never their Lord, because they never actually submitted to Him as Lord by living in accordance with His teaching. Instead, they did what they felt in their heart was God's will. Therefore Christ will reject them, declaring them to be workers of partiality.

The teaching from the devil is that people are regarded as right [justified] in God's sight, through living in accordance with what they feel in their heart is right. For the serpent told Eve that she would not die i.e. not suffer spiritual separation from God, due to eating the forbidden fruit, but that she and Adam would actually become as gods, knowing good and evil. What is subtly implied by the devil is that since people have become somewhat like God, in that we now inherently know what is good and what is evil, we are therefore capable of knowing what is righteous and what is unrighteous, without having them defined for us by God. Yet God's Word clearly teaches that knowledge concerning unrighteousness came to people via the Mosaic Law, and that knowledge concerning righteousness comes to people via God's Word apart from the Mosaic Law. Gen 3:4-5; Rom 1:16-17; 3:21; 7:7; Gal 2:21.

Christ will disavow those people who do what they feel in their heart is right rather than live in accordance with His teaching. For although many will profess that they know Christ, by emphatically calling Him Lord, and even prophesying, casting out demons, and doing many wonderful works in His name, they actually deny Him - who He is - by not living in accordance with His teaching. And whoever denies Christ before men, will likewise be denied by Christ before His heavenly Father. Matt 10:33; 2 Tim 2:12; Titus 1:16.

Let us therefore be followers of God, as dear children. And walk in love, as Christ also has loved us i.e. without respect of persons, and has given himself for us, an offering and a sacrifice to God, which is pleasing to Him. But physical or religious fornication, moral or religious impurity, and the desire to possess things that belong to others, let them not be once named among you who have become godly at heart. Nor talking favourably about physical or religious fornication, nor laughing about impure morals or religion, nor joking about desiring to possess things that belong to others. But rather, the giving of thanks to God for what we have. For this you know, that no one who commits physical or religious fornication, no one who practices impure morals or religion, and no one who desires to possess things that belong to others, who is a person who loves the world and is therefore spiritually adulterous towards God, has any inheritance in the eternal kingdom of Christ, the kingdom of God. Eph 5:1-5.

See then that you walk with caution, not as fools, but as wise, redeeming the time, because the days are full of self-centeredness, which is evil. Therefore be not unwise, but rather, understanding what the will of the Lord is. Eph 5:15-17.

Let no one deceive themselves. If anyone among you seems to be wise concerning this world, let them become a fool concerning this world, so that they may be wise concerning God's will. For the wisdom of this world is foolishness with God. For it is written that God takes the wise in their own craftiness, and that the Lord knows the thoughts of the wise concerning this world, that they are unproductive. 1 Cor 3:18-20.

Submit yourselves therefore to God. Resist the devil, and he will flee from you. Draw near to God, and He will draw near to you. Cleanse your hands, you sinners, and purify your hearts, you double minded. Be afflicted, and mourn, and weep. Let your laughter be turned to mourning, and your joy to heaviness. Humble yourselves in the sight of the Lord, and He will lift you up. Jas 4:7-10.

Now I beseech you, brethren, mark them that cause divisions and offences contrary to the teaching that you have learned - via the New Testament to God's will - and avoid them. For such people do not serve our Lord Jesus Christ. Instead, they gratify their own worldly desires. And by good words and fair speeches they deceive the hearts of those less wise than others and therefore easier deceived. Rom 16:17-18.

Study God's Word to show yourself approved unto God, a workman that need not be ashamed, rightly dividing the word of truth. And shun opinionated and unproductive nonsense. For they will increase unto more ungodliness. Yet the foundation of God - Christ's gospel concerning God's eternal kingdom - stands sure, having this seal, The Lord knows them that are His i.e. those who have deeply and unreservedly accepted His gospel. And, let everyone who professes to be one of Christ's - a Christian - depart from partiality. 2 Tim 2:15-19.

God's word apart from the Mosaic Law says that every person's way is right in their own eyes. And that the human heart is deceitful above all things, and desperately wicked. So deceitful in fact is the human heart, that God's Word goes on to emphasize the point that the human heart cannot be trusted as a guide to what is righteous and unrighteous, by posing the question, Who can know it? Then bearing the answer, I the LORD. For only God can comprehend the human heart. Hence whoever does what they feel in their heart to be right, is a fool, being self-deceived, whereas whoever trusts wholeheartedly in God's Word apart from the Mosaic Law, is wise, and will be regarded as right [justified] in God's sight. Prov 16:2; 21:2; 28:26; Jer 17:9-10.

24-27 Therefore whosoever heareth these sayings of mine, and doeth them, I will liken him unto a wise man, which built his house upon a rock: And the rain descended, and the floods came, and the winds blew, and beat upon that house; and it fell not: for it was founded upon a rock. And every one that heareth these sayings of mine, and doeth them not, shall be likened unto a foolish man, which built his house upon the sand: And the rain descended, and the floods came, and the winds blew, and beat upon that house; and it fell: and great was the fall of it.

Therefore, whoever hears the preceding teaching of Christ and lives in accordance with it, in essence and in honesty, is like a wise man who built his hope of a testament to God's will on a sound foundation. So when the devil sends unjustifiable criticism, victimization, and slander, their testament will stand because it is built upon Christ, God's Word incarnate - the New Testament to God's will. Jn 4:23-24; Gal 5:5; Lk 6:46-48.

Conversely, whoever hears the preceding teaching of Christ and yet does not live in accordance with it, in essence and honesty, is like a foolish man who built his hope of a testament to God's will on an unsound foundation. So when the devil sends unjustifiable criticism, victimization, and slander, their testament will fall because it is built upon what they feel in their heart is God's will. Lk 6:49.

Metaphorically speaking: Man's feeling is the essence of Thorny Ground. Therefore whoever keeps the devil's teaching in their heart is Thorny Ground.

Summary

We must exclusively keep Christ's teaching, in order to be justified - regarded as personally righteous in God's sight. Rom 12:16; 2 Jn 1:9; Prov 3:5; Gal 3:6; Jas 2:21-24; Philip 3:9.

Chapter Six

THE SUPREME AUTHORITY

Jesus Christ

John 1:1 & 14; Revelation 19:13 & 16.

Christ, the Author of Salvation

Do not be ashamed of Christ's gospel concerning God's eternal kingdom, for it is the power of God unto salvation to everyone who believes. Rom 1:16.

As every man has received the gift i.e. has freely and impartially received God's Spirit of graciousness contained within Christ, even so minister the same, one to another - freely and impartially - as good stewards of the manifold graciousness of God. For it is by God's Spirit of graciousness dwelling within, condemning unrighteousness to death in the flesh and working to do righteousness, that people are saved. 1 Pet 4:10; Eph 2:8; 3:7-8; 1 Cor 1:4; Jas 4:6; Jn 1:14 & 17.

If any man speaks, let him speak as the sayings of God. If any man minister God's Word, let him do it as of the ability that God gives - i.e. the ability to gain and utilize the knowledge and understanding specifically from Christ's teaching - so that God in all things may be glorified through Jesus Christ, to whom be praise and dominion for ever and ever. Amen. 1 Pet 4:11; 2 Cor 3:6.

You trusted in Christ, after you heard the Word of Truth, the gospel of your salvation - Christ's gospel concerning God's eternal kingdom. And you were sealed in Christ, after you believed, sealed with that Holy Spirit of promise i.e. God's

Spirit of graciousness, which is the assurance of the future redemption of your soul, to the praise of God's glory. Eph 1:13-14; 2 Tim 2:10; 1 Jn 5:11; Jn 1:14; 1 Cor 6:19-20.

And being made perfect, He became the author of eternal salvation to all them that obey him, Christ, God's Word incarnate. Heb 5:9.

Christ, the New Testament to God's Will

God, who at various times and in different manners spoke in times past to the forefathers by the prophets and mediators of the Old Testament to God's will, has in these last days spoken to us by his Son, the Lord Jesus Christ, the mediator of New Testament to God's will. Heb 1:1-2.

Therefore we ought to give the more earnest heed to the things that we have heard spoken to us by the Lord Jesus Christ, lest at any time we should let them slip. For if the word spoken by angels, via Moses and the prophets of the Old Testament, was steadfast, and every transgression and disobedience to that word received a just recompense of reward i.e. physical death without mercy, then how shall we escape a much sorer punishment i.e. spiritual death without mercy, if we, in spite of God's Spirit of graciousness dwelling within us, neglect so great salvation, which was first spoken by the Lord Jesus Christ in person, and then confirmed to us by the writers of the New Testament. Heb 2:1-3; 10:28-29.

For we know Him that has said, Vengeance belongs to Me, I will recompense, says the Lord. And, The Lord Jesus Christ shall judge his people. It is a fearful thing to fall into the hands of the living God. Heb 10:30-31.

The Lord Jesus Christ is the mediator of the New Testament to God's will. Heb 9:15.

Christ, the Reason for Opposition

Beloved, think it not strange concerning the fiery trial that is to try your faith, as though some strange thing happened to you. But rejoice, because you are partakers of Christ's sufferings, so that when his glory shall be revealed, you may be glad also with exceeding joy. If you are falsely accused for the name of Christ, then you are blessed. For the spirit of glory and of God rests upon you. By those reproaching you, Christ is evil spoken of. But by you suffering the reproach, Christ is glorified. None of you is to be a murderer, or a thief, or an evildoer, or a busybody in other people's matters, and therefore suffer the consequences. But if anyone suffers as a Christian - for living in accordance with Christ's teaching - let him not be ashamed. Instead, let him glorify God because of it. 1 Pet 4:12-16.

For the time has come that judgment must begin at the house of God. And if it first begins at us - who obey Christ's gospel of the kingdom - then what shall the end be of them who do not obey Christ's gospel? And if the righteous scarcely be saved, where shall the ungodly and the sinner appear? Therefore let them that suffer fiery trial of their faith, commit the keeping of their souls to God, by being faithful to Christ, as to a faithful Creator. 1 Pet 4:17-19; Rom 8:28.

Christ's gospel concerning God's kingdom shall be preached in the entire world for a witness to all nations. And then the end will come. Matt 24:14; Mk 1:14-15.

Christ, the Validation of Faith

Examine yourselves, whether or not you are in the faith i.e. whether or not your fruit / works validate your faith in Christ, God's Word incarnate. Prove your own selves, whether or not

God's Spirit of graciousness and truth dwells within you. Do you not know your own selves, how that Jesus Christ, God's Word incarnate, full of grace and truth, is in you spiritually unless you are reprobates? i.e. unless you are unprincipled, in that you do not have within you the fundamental truth of Christ's gospel - that all people must now be reconciled to God by faith in Christ as the sacrificial Lamb, and regarded as right in God's sight by faithfulness to Christ as the resurrected Lord. 2 Cor 13:5; Rom 8:9-16; Jn 1:14; Philip 1:19; Gal 5:22-25; Jer 6:30.

Faith, if it does not have works, is dead, being alone. By works - done by faith - a person is justified, and not by faith only i.e. not by faith alone. Jas 2:17 & 24; Heb 11:8.

Christ, the Confirmation of Our Salvation

Let us hear the conclusion of the whole matter: Fear God, and keep His commandments. For this is the whole duty of man. For God shall bring every work into judgment, with every secret thing, whether it be gracious or self-centered. Eccles 12:13-14.

And this is God's commandment, via the New Testament to His will, That we should believe on the name of His Son Jesus Christ, and love one another, as Christ gave us commandment i.e. trust and obey Christ. 1 Jn 3:23.

We know that we have passed from death to life, by the fact that we bear kindness and consideration [love] towards all people irrespective of persons, as Christ gave us commandment. 1 Jn 3:14-15; Matt 5:44-48; Jas 2:8-9.

If anyone says that they love God, and yet intentionally bears meanness and inconsideration [hate] towards a fellow human being, they are a liar. For whoever does not love their fellow human being whom they have seen, how can they love God whom they have not seen? And this commandment we have from God, That whoever loves God is to love their fellow human being also. 1 Jn 4:20-21.

These things I have written to you who believe on the Lord Jesus Christ, so that you may know that you have eternal life, and so that you may believe with confidence on the Lord Jesus Christ. 1 Jn 5:13-14.

Therefore, my beloved, as you have always obeyed the Lord Jesus Christ, not only in my presence, but now much more in my absence, work out your own salvation with fear and trembling. For it is God that works in you - by His Spirit of graciousness contained within Christ's teaching - both to will and to do His good pleasure. Philip 2:10-13; 1 Jn 4:13.

Chapter Seven

OUR COMPLETE SALVATION

Jesus Christ

Ephesians 6:10-18.

Christ's Power to Redeem

Finally, my brethren, be strong in the Lord Jesus Christ, and in the power of his might - His almighty ability to redeem people from the curse of the Mosaic Law and from all partiality. Eph 6:10; Jn 1:12-14; Gal 3:13; Titus 2:14; Heb 9:15; Rom 4:25.

Put on the whole armour of God - the entirety of God's Word incarnate, the New Testament to God's will, which is complete in itself - so that you may be able to maintain your sacred duty on this temporary earth, against the devil's devices. Eph 6:11; Rom 13:14.

For we do not wrestle against flesh and blood - the people who falsely accuse, unjustifiably criticise, victimize, and slander us - but against principalities, powers, and the rulers of spiritual ignorance and misunderstanding of this world. We wrestle against spiritual wickedness in high places, which operate through people, by sending them to falsely accuse, unjustifiably criticise, victimize, and slander us. Eph 6:12; Col 2:8-10.

Therefore take to yourself the whole armour of God - the entirety of God's Word incarnate, the New Testament to God's will, which is complete in itself - so that you may be able to withstand the devil's devices when he attacks you, and not fail personally in doing God's will, while endeavouring to declare it to others. Eph 6:13; 1 Cor 9:27; 10:12; 2 Pet 3:17-18.

Stand therefore, and maintain your sacred duty on this temporary earth, against the devil's devices, by applying the following...

Christ, Our Defence against Disloyalty

Stand against the devil's devices, by having your loins girt about with truth, that is, by having your honest mind strengthened often with the knowledge concerning God's will specifically from Christ's teaching. Eph 6:14; 1 Pet 1:13; 2Pet 1:5.

For if you were to lack knowledge concerning God's will, then you would be in danger of abandoning Christ's gospel concerning God's eternal kingdom, and then having the gospel disintegrate within you.

Metaphorically speaking: Good Ground must have its cohesive core strengthened often with new rain. For if it were to lack rain, then it would be in danger of falling away from the farmer's seed, and then having the seed decompose within it.

Christ, Our Defence against Deceptiveness

Stand against the devil's devices, by having on the breastplate of righteousness, that is, by having your good heart safeguarded often with the understanding concerning God's will specifically from Christ's teaching. Eph 6:14; 2 Pet 1:6-7.

For if you were to lack understanding concerning God's will, then you would be in danger of depriving your new spiritual life of nourishment, and inevitably producing a bad example of God's will.

Metaphorically speaking: Good Ground must have its pure core safeguarded often with new rain. For if it were to lack rain, then it would be in danger of depriving its plant of nourishment, and inevitably bearing bad fruit.

Christ, Our Defence against Stumbling

Stand against the devil's devices, by having your feet shod with the preparation of the gospel of peace, that is, by having your ability to walk in accordance with God's will protected with the willingness to be reconciled with all people who cause you suffering. Eph 6:15; Lk 17:3-4.

For if you lack the willingness to forgive those who offend you, then you are in danger of personally failing to do God's will, while endeavouring to preach it to others. Matt 6:15; 1 Cor 9:27.

Christ, Our Defence against Accusation

Above all, stand by taking the shield of faith by which you will be able to quench all the fiery darts of the wicked, that is, by having deep conviction for Christ, God's Word incarnate - the New Testament to God's will - so that you can thereby endure all the false accusations fired at you by the devil because of your testament to God's will. Eph 6:16.

For false accusation is the devil's device by which he endeavours to burn up your testament to God's will.

Metaphorically speaking: Fiery darts are the devil's device by which he endeavours to burn up your plant or house which glorifies God.

Christ, Our Defence against Persecution

And stand by taking the helmet of salvation, and the sword of the Spirit, which is the word of God, that is, by ensuring that you have wisdom from God concerning salvation, and also the full assurance of spiritual understanding, which is the very essence of God's Word. In other words, persistently ask God for wisdom concerning His will, diligently seek the knowledge concerning God's will specifically from Christ's teaching, and patiently ponder the Truth you find in Christ's teaching throughout the New Testament, with unreserved conviction, so that you can thereby endure all the unjustifiable criticism, victimization, and slander, sent upon you by the devil because of your new spiritual life. Eph 6:17; Col 2:2; Jn 14:17; 17:17.

For unjustifiable criticism, victimization, and slander, are the devil's devices by which he endeavours to undermine your new spiritual life.

Metaphorically speaking: Rain, floods, and winds, are the devil's devices by which he endeavours to undermine your plant or house which glorifies God.

Christ's Power to Uphold

And finally, stand against the devil's devices by always praying with all your prayers and pleas in accordance with the essence of Christ's teaching, and taking care to do so for all Christians, as opposed to selfishly praying just for yourself and those

Christians that you know of. Eph 6:18; 1 Pet 1:5; 2 Tim 2:3-4.

For every Christian is a fellow soldier in Christ's army, and is dependent on Christ to uphold them in their sacred duty to God, against the principalities, powers, and rulers of spiritual ignorance and misunderstanding of this world. Therefore, when praying to God, ensure that your requests are for every member of Christ's army - as per the Lord's prayer [see chapter four] - rather than just for yourself and those members that you know of.

CHART

Get your copy of the large full-colour companion chart, via:

Email: witback@gmail.com
or
Download: https://flic.kr/s/aHskZnXBzH

See the following two piece sample copy. The actual chart, via download or email, comes in two high resolution A4 size printer friendly pieces.

Please write a positive review of this book and chart on Amazon. Reviews are extremely important. So please do write one. Thank you.

The Seven Phases

The Four Responses to Christ's Gospel of God's Kingdom

INSEMINATION / SOWING	CONCEPTION / ABSORPTION	IMPLANTATION / GERMINATION
1	2	3

4 THE CONTRITE at HEART deeply and unreservedly accept Christ's Gospel concerning God's kingdom, and thus support and nurture it. They hear, understand, and in an honest and good heart keep God's Word, and produce a good example of God's will. Matt 13:23; Mk 4:20; Lk 8:15. THE GOOD GROUND receives the Seed, and brings forth fruit. Matt 13:8; Mk 4:8; Lk 8:8.

GOSPEL — CONTRITE HEART — SEED — GOOD GROUND

PREVIOUS SPIRITUAL BELIEF — PREVIOUS RAIN

FUNDAMENTAL TRUTH — PRIMARY ROOT

3 THE RESERVED at HEART deeply yet reservedly accept Christ's Gospel, and thus inevitably deprive their new life. They hear God's Word, but worldly cares, riches, and lusts, choke them, and they bring no fruit to perfection. Matt 13:22; Mk 4:18-19; Lk 8:14. THE THORNY GROUND receives the Seed, but thorns grow with it, and choke it. Matt 13:7; Mk 4:7; Lk 8:7.

GOSPEL — RESERVED HEART — SEED — THORNY GROUND

PREVIOUS SPIRITUAL BELIEF — PREVIOUS RAIN

FUNDAMENTAL TRUTH — FEELINGS — PRIMARY ROOT — THORN ROOTS

2 THE SUPERFICIAL at HEART shallowly accept Christ's Gospel, and thus soon abandon it. They hear God's Word, but have no root, and thus fall away when trouble or persecution arises due to the word. Matt 13:20-21; Mk 4:16-17; Lk 8:13. THE STONY GROUND receives the Seed, but has no root, and thus falls away when the sun rises, because they lack moisture. Matt 13:5-6; Mk 4:5-6; Lk 8:6.

GOSPEL — SUPERFICIAL HEART — SEED — STONY GROUND

NO SPIRITUAL BELIEF — NO RAIN

INSUFFICIENT TRUTH — OPINIONS — INADEQUATE ROOT — STONES

1 THE STUBBORN at HEART instantly refuse Christ's Gospel concerning God's kingdom. They hear God's Word, but do not understand it. Then Satan takes it away, lest they believe and be saved. Matt 13:19; Mk 4:15; Lk 8:12. THE WAY SIDE refuses the Seed, and it is trodden down, and then birds come and eat it up. Matt 13:4; Mk 4:4; Lk 8:5.

GOSPEL — STUBBORN HEART — SEED — THE WAYSIDE

The Seven Phases of Spi

1 Endowed with God's favour [Blessed] are people
2 Endowed with God's favour [Blessed] are people
3 Endowed with God's favour [Blessed] are people
4 Endowed with God's favour [Blessed] are people
5 Endowed with God's favour [Blessed] are people
6 Endowed with God's favour [Blessed] are people
7 Endowed with God's favour [Blessed] are people

# of Spiritual Development

GESTATION / NOURISHMENT	TALKING / LEAF BEARING	LIVING / FRUIT BEARING	TEACHING / SEED BEARING

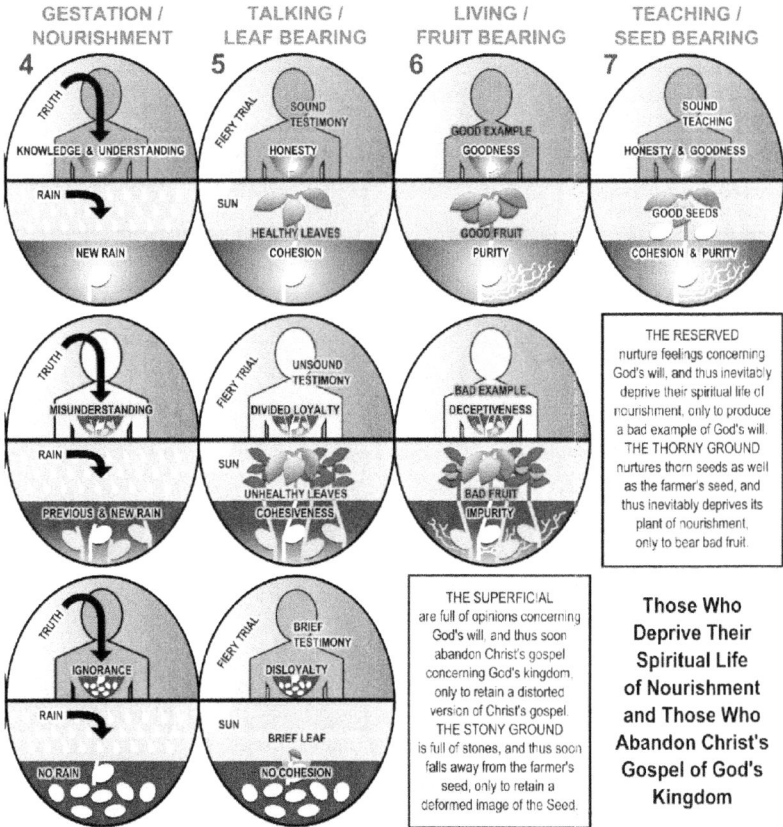

4

TRUTH

KNOWLEDGE & UNDERSTANDING

RAIN

NEW RAIN

5

FIERY TRIAL

SOUND TESTIMONY

HONESTY

SUN

HEALTHY LEAVES

COHESION

6

GOOD EXAMPLE

GOODNESS

GOOD FRUIT

PURITY

7

SOUND TEACHING

HONESTY & GOODNESS

GOOD SEEDS

COHESION & PURITY

TRUTH

MISUNDERSTANDING

RAIN

PREVIOUS & NEW RAIN

FIERY TRIAL

UNSOUND TESTIMONY

DIVIDED LOYALTY

SUN

UNHEALTHY LEAVES

COHESIVENESS

BAD EXAMPLE

DECEPTIVENESS

BAD FRUIT

IMPURITY

THE RESERVED nurture feelings concerning God's will, and thus inevitably deprive their spiritual life of nourishment, only to produce a bad example of God's will. THE THORNY GROUND nurtures thorn seeds as well as the farmer's seed, and thus inevitably deprives its plant of nourishment, only to bear bad fruit.

TRUTH

IGNORANCE

RAIN

NO RAIN

FIERY TRIAL

BRIEF TESTIMONY

DISLOYALTY

SUN

BRIEF LEAF

NO COHESION

THE SUPERFICIAL are full of opinions concerning God's will, and thus soon abandon Christ's gospel concerning God's kingdom, only to retain a distorted version of Christ's gospel. THE STONY GROUND is full of stones, and thus soon falls away from the farmer's seed, only to retain a deformed image of the Seed.

Those Who Deprive Their Spiritual Life of Nourishment and Those Who Abandon Christ's Gospel of God's Kingdom

ritual Development

Matt 5:3-9, Mk 1:14 -15.

who are contrite and deeply and unreservedly accept Christ's gospel concerning God's eternal kingdom.

who then become mournful due to Christ's gospel consuming their previous spiritual belief.

who then become fully and exclusively submissive to the fundamental truth of Christ's gospel.

who then genuinely desire knowledge and understanding concerning God's will.

who then support and nurture their new life's potential to consistently produce a sound testimony to God's will.

who then go on to nurture their new life's potential to actual produce a good example of God's will.

who then go on to nurture their new life to maturity, capable of impartially producing sound teaching concerning God's will.

Another book by this author:

God's Guide to The End Times: The Revelation of Jesus Christ in Plain English.

Read in plain English what God has revealed concerning the end of the world, including:
- The intense trial that is coming upon the world to clarify the faith of unfaithful Christians - And how we can avoid it.
- The terrible trouble that is coming upon the world to prove the defiance of unrepentant people - And why they will not escape it.
- The divine judgement that awaits every person to decide the destiny of all humanity - And exactly who will go where, when and why.

The clearest and truest reiteration of Christ's revelation concerning the end times.

Includes giant full colour companion chart, in seven A4 size printer friendly pieces, via download or email.

Printed in Great Britain
by Amazon

46072060R00057